HOW TO START ON A SHOESTRING
AND
MAKE A PROFIT WITH HYDROPONICS

Including set-up, production and maintenance, and marketing

By
Hilmur L. Saffell

Third edition, completely revised

Mayhill Press, Franklin, Tennessee

HOW TO START ON A SHOESTRING AND MAKE A PROFIT WITH HYDROPONICS

Including setup, production and maintenance, and marketing

By Hilmur L. Saffell

Published by:
Mayhill Press
PO Box 681804
Franklin, TN 37068-1804

Publisher's Cataloging in Publication Data
Saffell, Hilmur L.
How to Start on a Shoestring and Make a Profit with Hydroponics
Hilmur L. Saffell - 3rd edition, completely rev.
    136 pp, illus., bibliography
1. Hydroponics
2. Indoor Gardening
3. Home Business
4. Entrepreneurship
            631.58 SAF   LCN: 93-78759
ISBN - 0-9637066-3-2, Softcover, 8 1/2 x 11

TABLE OF CONTENTS

PREFACE

This book describes in detail how to get into the lucrative field of hydroponics without a large initial capital outlay. It is divided into two main sections: the Basic Startup section and the Commercial section. The reader is advised to carefully read the entire text before making any decisions for action. He is particularly advised to read the chapter on marketing.

At the start we give you information about the advantages and disadvantages of hydroponic culture, a survey of various approaches to hydroponics, and what you need to begin.

First we have to find a cheaper, more effective way to help the average individual get into hydroponics. This book proposes to do just that. From a "crude" rough start we will outline the materials and action which are needed to make a profit from the very beginning. In this section we will also discuss what factors lead to success, what to do when factors are not so favorable, and how to make-do in almost any situation.

Production and marketing will outline the continuing build-up toward a more sophisticated operation. What to do under differing circumstances. How to seed and how to produce plants from cuttings. What nutrient solutions to use. How to handle the weather. What plants to grow for the most profit. What to watch for and how to overcome deficiencies in plants.

We shall be talking about the important process of testing. We shall explain how to maintain and correct pH, and much more.

Marketing is the most important chapter. Marketing is what you must know before you begin. We will discuss the techniques needed to develop one's market. Tips on what you must do before you grow a crop. What to grow in order to meet the market's demand at a proper and profitable time. Ideas on where to find that market. Why packaging is a good idea. And finally, the future of hydroponics and how it may effect you.

In the Commercial section, you'll get down to details for making your first hydroponicum. Here you are shown how to construct a first-rate greenhouse from scratch with inexpensive materials. You are shown a breakdown in costs and profit - where it is possible, with diligence and dedication for two people to earn a good living on as little as 1/3 acre. Many other topics are covered, such as : lights and lighting, extra carbon dioxide for faster growth, computers in greenhouses, the culture of various crops including tomatoes and cucumbers, tissue culture, different media techniques, how to save on energy and labor.

SECTION ONE:

THE BASIC STARTUP

CHAPTER 1

THE TRUTH ABOUT HYDROPONICS

The world is getting more and more crowded. Millions are already starving. And here in the United States our day has just about arrived. We have washed away most of our topsoil, we have flushed what's left with "chemicals" and pesticides. We have literally thrown away the breadbasket of the world.

The prophets of the soil say that hydroponics will not solve our problems. But since there is not much soil to speak of, these critics offer few valid solutions to our problems. It is our belief that if there is a future for us on this planet, hydroponics will play a large part in it.

Whenever a crop is lost hydroponically, a great to-do is made of it. But if a farmer loses a crop with soil culture he just starts planning for next year's crop. A lot of fuss is also made over the high cost of growing plants hydroponically. The soil enthusiasts fail to explain how much it costs them to buy equipment, land, buildings and labor to continue growing in the old way. A fair comparison must be made. A sophisticated hydroponic installation is no more expensive than a larger area of land farmed in the usual way. In fact it is somewhat cheaper! Once installed, a hydroponicum, compared to soil farming, needs very little attention. It is very efficient and requires just a little labor to keep it going at an optimum rate. A hydroponicum uses less fertilizer, much less water, and can be erected anywhere. Even on rock and cement!

We also have those who say that hydroponics is too complicated, that it requires accurate attention, that it needs good housekeeping, that it cannot be used for growing field crops such as rice, corn or wheat. Hydroponics is not complicated. It does require good housekeeping. It does require attention. But what business venture, if it is to be profitable, does not require all of these? And Hindus do grow rice hydroponically; Australian's grow hay.

In other words, you need to pay attention to detail and use your common sense. Once you have a large hydroponicum, you can hire someone with a chemical background to keep track of things. You don't have to be a chemist yourself. Nobody can be all things.

Hydroponic experts now agree that hydroponics is practical, that it is profitable in most situations and that the possibilities for soilless production of crops is endless. Using the method this book proposes, you will find hydroponics inexpensive to set up and maintain. You will have economical crop production with greatly increased output. This will be particularly true with flowers. They will bloom 3-4 weeks earlier and give you a longer cutting season. Hydroponics is not a hit-or-miss affair as it is with soil culture. Soil changes from time to time; no accurate continuing analysis can be made of it. Each batch of soil differs drastically. Not to mention the weather and other factors completely out of one's control. With hydroponics you have complete control. You know exactly what's going on, you can depend upon yourself and what you know. Hydroponics is like what the ideal soil should be without soil's handicaps.

So what are the advantages of "farming" hydroponically? Without soil, without humus, without manure? You will find the following to be true:

...higher yield per area used...no soil disease...faster growth...plants can be closer together (roots don't have to forage so far to get necessary nutrients)...operating and maintenance costs are much lower...little manual labor needed...no big expensive machinery...no weeds...no manures or contagion...fruits and flowers of excellent quality...fruits and vegetables with special mineral content for specific diet needs...less fertilizer needed, less water used, less waste...no long waiting period, an immediate return...can be maintained indefinitely at a very low cost...no crop rotation needed...no erosion, no drought, no monsoons...pests and bugs kept to the very minimum...

What are the disadvantages?

...you must stick to detail because the margin for error is greater than it is with soil...the need for constant learning as you progress and become larger in your operation...

These are the same "disadvantages' one must overcome in any business venture. The larger your business becomes, the more you need to know in order to get the job done. Even a successful soil or farming operation requires the same attention and know-how.   With hydroponics you can determine what the final product will be in appearance and nutritional quality. Which makes for a higher price in the market. Flower and keeping qualities are much better. Two people, say man and wife, need work only 20 hours each per month to start and keep a 1/3 acre hydroponic setup in operation. This leaves plenty of time for marketing, the prime essential in any business.

Which brings us to that old argument: organic versus chemical. There is absolutely no evidence, scientific or otherwise, that fruits and vegetables (certainly not flowers and foliage) grown hydroponically are of any less value in nutrition or appearance than those grown in soil. In many cases hydroponic vegetables are sweeter and have more flavor.

Chemical fertilizers come from the earth (where else?). They are derived from organic products. There is essentially no difference between them and organic manures. Plants grow a lot faster and better because soil makes available to plants only a small percentage of the chemicals needed for growth. Forty per cent of moisture in the soil is unavailable to plants. Chemicals applied directly do not have to go through changes in order for the plant to utilize them. Therefor we can have faster and more vigorous growth. The humus in soil holds water for bacteria to use and then present chemicals in a proper form to plants. Hydroponics skips the bacterial middleman and makes the food available directly.

In any case the argument between "organic" or "chemical" is academic. There is no other way to go. We have used up our resources. Hydroponics is the last best hope for a world worn-out from over-production. You, as a grower, will be doing a great service not only for yourself but also for mankind. According to your desires, you will be able to grow nutritious vegetables, wondrous flowers, and perhaps eventually fine grains in quantity. You will do all of this without tearing up the earth, without waste, without pollution. Given the correct attention and growing conditions, hydroponics can furnish crops to help feed a hungry world.

Let's say it again: what you need is common sense and some gardening knowledge. You already know that too much "love" is not good for plants. So, in all your dealings with plants, let them be your guide - they will tell you what's needed. Start slow - get the feel of it. Don't borrow money at the outset. Grow crops with which you are familiar. Know your markets. Grow the higher-priced fast growing crops. Keep a part of your profits in reserve to finance expansion. Run your hydroponicum like a factory. Do not over-produce. As much as possible, keep your operation going all year round. Do not waste time or space. Get to where you can reasonably forecast your crops within 10% for each and every year.

****

In Standard, Ca a five acre hydroponicum furnishes premium tomatoes and European cucumbers at above market prices to the better hotels and restaurants in the San Francisco area.

At Plant City, Fl, a grower raises vegetables like the growers do in Israel. The Florida grower works with beds of fine gray sand which has very little organic material in it. This is like having crops in sand/gravel beds, only these beds are nearly 1,000 acres large!

The idea was started by people at a power plant. Water from the adjacent East river is pumped into the generating bouse and through a heat exchanger. The water is then piped to the blanket which surrounds the generators' lubricating oil. Here the water picks up the excess heat and is then run into the greenhouse. Another heat exchanger converts the water's heat through a closed loop where fans distribute the heat throughout the greenhouse. Thus with a significant savings in heating bills, the power house utilizes waste heat which was formerly pumped back into the East river but which now helps grow lettuce, tomatoes, cucumbers and other vegetables.

CHAPTER 2

SETTING UP YOUR FIRST HYDROPONICUM

Hydroponics (growing in water) is a system which needs a medium wherein plants can anchor themselves. The following are also basic needs: a feeding mix (wet or dry), ample light, protection from bad weather. There are several ways to set up a hydroponic operation. The one we propose for beginners is our own variation of the Bengal System which was first explained by Douglas Sholto.

This system is very easy to start up. Using native materials it can be set up anywhere. It is very productive and it is easy to maintain.

For those who want to start out on a more advanced basis, we shall explain the Bag technique at the end of this Basic Section. And in Section Two we shall discuss the NFT and other systems as well as more advanced data on sand and gravel techniques. Regardless of the system you use, the principle is still the same: keep the medium moist like a wrung-out sponge. With the Bengal system we fertilize and water by hand. The modern hydroponist does the same - differing only in that he uses an injection system to feed and water the medium and the plants. Your goal, as this book suggests, is to go from using only your hands to a greenhouse which is automated. In the beginning you won't even have a greenhouse to work with. That all comes later. Information in Section One will be sufficient for most start-up operators, but for those who really want to grow, Section Two will cover just about anything you'd want to know in hydroponics.

What are the site factors for a Hydroponic Operation?

Of course you need some land. You must have available water, close proximity to your media (in this case sand and gravel), ample labor when the time comes. You should be fairly near your markets to ensure freshness of product. Until you get a greenhouse, your local climate will dictate what crops you grow. Average rainfall and prevailing winds will enter into this. Nearness to suppliers and a power supply are also very important.

To start you can gain some operating capital if you have some 1500 square feet of unused garden space. Do this by planting garlic or shallots no more than 2 1/2 inches apart in all directions within the prescribed space. In most areas plant in September and harvest in June. If you live too far North, plant early in the year and harvest as late as you can.

Garlic sells at a fairly high price; shallots sell even higher. Sell directly to the retail market and make your own deal. Try for 2/3 of their retail to determine your wholesale price. Your crops should average 1 1/2 pounds per square foot, giving a total of 2250 pounds. You will have to compost and/or fertilize heavily to do this. But you're only going to do it for one or two years to get the extra cash. These are two "secret" vegetables which most people know nothing about. Still they are the easiest crops in the world to grow. They have no bugs, no diseases. Why not grow these vegetables hydroponically and increase our production even more? Because these vegetables need 6-8 months to mature. Commercial growers, as well as yourself, must stick to fast- growing crops - those which can mature or fruit within 3-4 months. And you want at least 3-4 crops per year! You can't waste time or space. You must shoot for the highest gross profit possible per square foot.

For the first year or so most of us will stick to the following plan: (a) "throw-away" beds for high priced vegetables and (b) potted flowers and foliage for bench crops. You should also research your local market to determine other items which might produce a good profit within the time limits we have imposed upon them.

The Throw-Away Bed:

This is a misnomer. These beds can last for years. Gravel and sand don't wear out; soil does. However, these beds are not as frugal with water and fertilizer as is the true hydroponicum. The standard bed is 90 feet by 5 feet and is 9 inches deep. If your pocketbook is limited, you can with a little ingenuity construct beds with what's at hand. If your pockets are bare, then scoop the above bed or trench out of the ground and line it with polythene plastic. Pack the bottom down fairly hard. Line the trench, both bottom and sides, with the polythene. Mil 6 thickness will do well but any reasonable thickness will serve your purpose.

If you live in an area of heavy rainfall you may have trouble with this type of bed because it will flood. Build a plastic shelter over the bed and dig drainage ditches around it. Your planting medium for this bed will consist of 5 parts crushed stone or pea gravel and 2-3 parts of sharp river sand. This kind of sand does not puddle when wet. If your area has dry weather use more sand than gravel. With wet weather use more gravel. The size of the gravel should be 1/4 to 5/8 inches in diameter. All stone and gravel should be thoroughly washed to remove silt and organic materials.

If you think this method is unusual or even old fashioned, there is an eleven acre plant doing just this and doing quite well - in Tucson, AZ. Like all systems, it has its advantages and disadvantages. Many of the larger operators recycle the nutrient. We don't recommend this for the individual who's starting out unless he's using the NFT technique.

Before we go any further let's talk about pH. This figure is simply the amount of hydrogen ions (the acid element) and hydroxyl ions (the alkaline element) in solution. If both hydrogen and hydroxyl ions comprise 50% each of the solution, then the pH is 7.0 or neutral. Less than 7.0 is an acid base; more than 7.0 is an alkaline base. Most plants like the pH to lie between 6.5 and 7.0. The gravel must be checked for pH. Calcareous gravel should be treated with superphosphate: 3 lbs to 100 gallons of water. Let this stand in beds overnight, drain, then re-fill and drain three times with fresh water. For sand, place a small quantity in a glass, add twice the sand's volume in distilled water, shake and settle. (You can do the same with gravel.) After a few minutes, take a pH reading with whatever pH kit you have at hand. Strips of litmus paper give an fairly accurate reading. The pH of the sand must be 7.0 or you will have to make adjustments after you install the sand in the beds. Don't forget to check the pH of your water supply before doing any of this.

Some rural water supplies can have a ph which is far from the norm and which would keep most plants from growing if used for watering and feeding. If you have city water, you can get an analysis of it by calling the water department. The people there will be quite happy to provide you with an analysis.

If you intend to stay with sand/gravel your beds will have to be more elaborate. Beds can be built with anything except galvanized iron. The zinc content in galvanized iron is toxic to plants. If you must use galvanized materials then paint them well with bituminous paint. If you should be using steel treat it to prevent corrosion because the nutrient solution will be slightly acidic. Beds can also be made from non-erodible mud plaster just as they're built in India.

Probably the best method for sand/gravel beds is to use corrugated asbestos cement roofing sheets. Cut these sheets to fit just the sides of the standard bed (90 ft by 5 ft by 9 inches deep). Interlock and bolt and then waterproof with polythene. Make certain the polythene walls are firmly attached to the tops of the sides. You can used wire clips for this. These beds should slope about 3 inches in their total length. At the downhill end, place a valve at the bottom for emergency draining. Dig a shallow ditch leading away from the valve and the bed area. Fancier beds of this sort will having piping inside the beds with slits along the bottom edge to take care of drainage. Use formaldehyde to sterilize the beds between crops. Aside from cleaning out all organic material left behind from pulled plants, you can use 1 part Formaline to 100 parts of water. Pump in enough to fill the beds just above the surface. Let this stand overnight. Cover the beds with plastic to hold the fumes. Workers must use masks while doing this. Drain completely the next day and flush out three times with fresh water.

Suppose you can't afford plastic housing at this time. Do like they do in India. If the beds become flooded during a heavy rain, simply open the valves and drain. If you still have plants in the beds and you want to cleanse with a simple flooding (no formaldehyde), open the drain. But close the drains immediately afterward and feed immediately to prevent starvation. It is hoped that you won't often be faced with this problem. Flooding of the beds for any reason is not a recommended procedure when plants are still growing in them. But sometimes it has to be done - insect infestation being one reason. Good housekeeping can prevent a lot of these kind of problems.

How many of these beds will be have?

One half of 1/3 acre will provide space for 20 beds, four to a "house", five houses in all. Two and a half houses will have beds; two and a half will have areas or benches for pots. That's the ideal startup. Actually you will have as many beds as you have time and space. Once these beds are in place, the hard work is over. The beds will require very little attention as far as upkeep and maintenance are concerned. Make sure you have at least 3 feet between the beds. You will need this space for walkways, working the beds, and the placing of polythene covers when income permits. All beds should run east and west - especially in the Northern half of the United States and also in Canada. Design everything for easy watering. An ordinary water hose will do in the beginning. Later on you can convert to PVC piping throughout. Do not use iron pipe because it corrodes.

As you can see, these "houses" or groups of beds will only be useful at this time for limited growing. Early spring, summer and late fall. Unless you live in the South. To start you won't be financially prepared to have an all-year house. The crops you plant will have to be harvested before hard winter comes. For the first year or so your operation will be in action for only 6-9 months. But this is still plenty of time to make a profit. The pot area will be laid out just like your beds - 90 ft long, 5 ft wide. Later you can have this area up on tables or planks to make it easier to work. Distance these tables 3 feet apart also. In this area you will grow flowers and foliage, usually in six inch pots.

This is the Basic Setup:

Always keep in mind you are the one who controls the weather. You control the moisture. You control the growth. Your plants will always need protection from sun, rain, hail and cold. At the start your setup will be quite rudimentary. As soon as possible you will have to erect protective shelter above the beds and the pots. This will entail the erection of PVC piping or penta-treated wood to construct a gable-like structure over the planted area.

The piping or wood should be anchored in the ground. The center height of the gable should be about 8 feet. This structure will be sufficient for the first year or two. Use a 10 gauge wire to hold up the plastic over the required distance. String it between upright supports about six feet apart. Use the cheapest materials you can find unless you intend to make this gravel/sand setup permanent. Run the wire parallel to the beds. Don't use wood supports in the beds; if you need to tie up plants tie them to the overhead wires. An excellent hail-resistant cover is polythene sheets with chicken wire sandwiched in between. You don't have to use this but it helps. Buy the polythene in 100 foot by 40 foot rolls from your supplier. Get the heaviest gauge you can afford - mil 6 or perhaps mil 12. Polythene will last about two years. If you spray the tops with water once a week, the polythene will last longer.

For those where winter is a problem, some solar heating will be required. An excellent passive system can be devised by lining the north side of each "house" with 55 gallon drums filled with water and painted black on the outside. You can also use plastic jugs of various sizes. Fill them with water and paint them black. Stack them on shelving as high as you can. The pathways between the beds should be covered with black plastic covered with an inch or two of soil. This extra protection will help extend your growing season in the fall and enable you to start earlier in the spring. You won't be able to go through the entire winter - not yet. So, to prevent freezing, let some water out of the drums and the plastic jugs. Another way to get seasonal growth extension is to plant "cool weather" plants, like lettuce and narcissus.

Be certain you have a way to vent your houses - if you've covered them on all sides with plastic sheeting. Sunny days will kill your plants unless you have adequate ventilation. Just pull up the sides of each house and tie the plastic with wire clips to the overhanging wire. You can get further ideas on this by viewing the greenhouse plans in Section Two of this book. Water lines must be insulated against the cold and in some areas against heat. If you are using an ordinary garden hose, you can turn it off at the tap or at the pump. If you are using PVC piping keep in mind while you're placing it what your future operation will be like. In all your planning think two years ahead. Place everything according to what you will be doing in that same space two years from now.

The Potting Shed:

Available nearby should be a small shed attached to a small greenhouse which has walls and a roof which have double sheets of mil 12 polythene hung two inches apart. The shed will be used for storage of fertilizer and potting materials. The greenhouse will be used for starting cuttings and seedlings. You can build a shed and a greenhouse for next to nothing. Use second hand or used lumber - often you can get it free of charge just for hauling it away.

You can heat the greenhouse with two heat lamps or spotlight bulbs focussed on the ground and hung about two feet high. This will do for the Southern states. For Northern states use a hot plate or electric space heater. Remember: gas fumes will kill plants. So be careful what kind of heating you use. The greenhouse should be eight feet at the center pole, five feet at the sides, twelve feet wide and up to fifteen feet long. Make your greenhouse out of used or second hand lumber. Both the shed and greenhouse should be placed on an east-west line, particularly in the Middle West and Northern states.

What are the first costs?

Costs will be sand and gravel, perhaps corrugated asbestos cement roofing sheets, six inch black plastic pots, some odds and ends. Most of the wood should be for free. You can get by without treated wood for the first two years. If you live in an area where the weather is mild, you can hold off on plastic for housing. You will need to get the shed and greenhouse up as soon as possible. These are the basic starting costs. As the profits come in you will begin to construct a more elaborate operation.

Find yourself a used concrete mixer - one of the smaller one-man sizes often seen at construction sites. You can rent one if you have to. This device will come in handy for mixing sand and gravel and also fertilizer. It will save you a lot of time and labor.

That's it, to start. This outline may not sound like the high technology you've heard about. But to tell the truth the amateur grower and beginner can get by quite nicely on the setup we have prescribed here. Later as the money comes in you can refer to Section Two to make your operation more sophisticated. But you can go a long way with the system already outlined here. Just choose your crops carefully, pay attention to growing requirements, and satisfy your

18

markets. Try to buy your six-inch pots from someone who has a lot of them on hand and will sell them for a low price. In this case, the last resort is to call your local or nearest supplier. You will need some flats for seedlings and cuttings. Make them yourself out of used lumber or whatever is at hand. In most cases you will have no need for intermediate size pots. Just go directly from the flats to the pots. After a while you will start out cuttings in the six inch pots. In every case try to simplify your operation and eliminate undue movement.

Use vermiculite for seedlings and cuttings. It's not cheap but a little goes a long way. For potting use a mixture of peat moss and vermiculite - about half and half. Use the pots for foliage and most flowering plants. Use the sand/gravel beds for vegetables and some flowers - like carnations and gladioli. Section Two includes a discussion on all sand or all gravel beds. We recommend the sand/gravel combination because it's cheap. We can hand feed and water in. We don't need sub-irrigation pipes. And, as you will discover toward the end of this section, although some growers start out with sand/gravel they usually end up with the bag technique. The commercial grower uses an injector system for feeding and watering - as eventually will you.

Why this technique?

As opposed to any other? Because sand/gravel is the lowest in cost. And it works! You will dry feed and water in. With conscientious behavior on your part, your beds and tables could yield the following. Spring and summer will see the beds with cantaloupe, honey dew melon and chili peppers; winter will see cauliflower, Brussels sprouts, leeks and lettuce. Or in summer the tables would have pots of ivy, pothos, mums. Fall and winter would have pots of African violets, gloxinia. Mid-winter will show up with hyacinth, daffodil and narcissus. Among the trees bordering your growing area or under lath shading you have constructed will be basket fern. A year or two from now those sand/gravel beds will be gone. A new hydroponicum will stand in their place.

****

In Mecca, Ca one gentleman has used an NFT technique for over 18 years. He uses no medium or sub-strate and grows his plants in water contained in cement troughs which cover three acres out in the open. That's correct. No greenhouse. And in desert country!

A hydroponicum in Orlando, FL features the Japanese system of floating styrofoam boards on the surface of a nutrient bath. The boards are 7 inches by 48 inches and 1 inch thick. They float on trays which are about 8 inches deep. The nutrient solution is constantly circulated and aerated. The boards are planted with seedlings at one end of the greenhouse and harvested at the other end.

CHAPTER 3

PRODUCTION AND MAINTENANCE

The most important thing to remember in running a hydroponicum is to plan your crops to follow one another. Never waste space; always have the beds full. Also keep accurate records on each crop, writing down every day what was fed and what you did. By doing this you will in time be able to choose the most profitable varieties you need to grow. You'll know what to expect of them and the actual cost of growing and preparing them for market. This makes good business sense. You would have to follow the same procedures in any other type of business - if you wanted to be successful.

Intercropping:

You'll plant twice as close in hydroponics as you once did in soil. You'll work more intensive - more so than the Chinese or the French methods used in soil culture. When growing winter crops, intercrop with lettuce or some other quick-growing cool-weather crop. By the time your major crop is coming into its own, the lettuce will have already been harvested and sold. Potted plants can be intercropped in the same way. The only factor you must observe in intercropping is the amount of light available to each and every plant. Some plants like shade - when small place them in the shade of the larger sun-loving plants. The leaves from some plants may be reduced when intercropping. This will not hurt the quality or quantity of fruit or bloom.

When intercropping in a sand/gravel bed you must take care that the pH is conducive to the growth of all plants in the bed. Usually a pH of 6.5 will be satisfactory. You can work within .2 either way and still be in okay. Once again your water supply must be adjusted for pH before using. Otherwise you will throw off all your pH readings.

Seeds and seedlings:

Seed vegetables directly into the beds by placing two seeds in each hole. At least one should sprout. For foliage and blooming plants, start in vermiculite trays and transplant to six inch pots. The best mixture for cuttings is 50% sharp river sand and 50% vermiculite. Cuttings need humidity, so make a plastic tent and drape it over the tray. Tap the surface of the tent now and then to drop the accumulated moisture back into the tray. Take the tent off once a week to examine the cuttings. In order to keep your pot area fully occupied with plants, you should be producing seedlings continuously in your potting shed. You can't have too many. Keep a close watch on the seedlings and cuttings, make sure they are all progressing at the same rate. Get them to the beds or pots as soon as possible.

Vermiculite will absorb just so much water. That's why it's good for seedlings and cuttings. Pre-soak it before using. Never use soil to start seeds - always use vermiculite. Soil has diseases - don't take the chance of introducing a disease to your hydroponicum and wiping out an entire crop. After your initial start, seedlings and cuttings should always be ready to take their places in areas where plants have been removed and sold.

Another success tip for the serious hydroponist: ALWAYS TEST YOUR SEED! This cannot be overstressed. Make germination tests of all seeds before planting. Put a piece of blotting paper on a saucer, place some seeds on it, cover with another piece of blotting paper which is damp. If the seed hasn't germinated in ten days, get rid of it! Another item: check for patents on plants before you grow them. Patents are copyrights; you have to have permission form the original owner. That takes money you can't afford to spend at this time.

Your seedling/cutting trays should be 3 inches deep. Their length and width should be what you can comfortably pick up in two hands. Most hydroponists suggest you don't feed seedlings or cuttings. The local success story in my area refutes that by using a weak Peter's Stem solution (suitable for the plant's needs) on all his cuttings. He must be right; his hydroponicum is a grand affair. To be on the safe side, you could follow his method with the cuttings but wait until the seedlings are 2 inches high before adding a weak solution of fertilizer.

The seedlings are now in their beds, the cuttings in their pots. Spread your dry feeding mixture at the rate of 1/2 ounce per square foot and a small pinch for each pot. Let water flow out over the bed until the bed is wet. (Remember to pre-soak the beds and pots and drain before planting.) If you think you've watered too heavily, let stand for a few minutes and then open the drain valve. Try not to get any moisture on the plants or their leaves. As the plants continue to grow - about a week later or in some cases just a few days - continue to add 1/2 ounce per square foot every 7-10 days. And of course water in. Between feedings, watering should take place every day, sometimes two or three times and more a day - depending on the temperature and the rate of evaporation. For the bag technique and all techniques which use a liquid solution for fertilization, use one tablespoon of fertilizer for each gallon of water. This is generally speaking; some plants require more and some less. Be sure to wet down the media until it is soaked.

It usually takes 1/4 to 1/2 gallon of water per square foot if the beds have been pre-soaked. Your situation may vary - so take notes and keep track of how the plants are doing. A fundamental principle of hydroponics is to use continuous weak feeding with intermittent flushing for accumulated salts.

With extreme alkaline water add sulfuric acid - 1/4 fluid ounce per 100 gallons. Pour the sulfuric acid very slowly into the water and do it outside in the open air. Do not breathe the fumes! **AND NEVER POUR THE WATER INTO THE SULFURIC ACID!** Devise a ratio of the two for the amount of water you are going to use. If you keep a close watch on the pH of your medium you will be able to cut down on excessive feeding. This will save fertilizer costs. Regularly check the pH of beds and also the elements of composition of the fertilizer. Just remember the pH has a tendency to drift toward alkalinity. Another item of real importance: iron cannot be properly absorbed by the plant when the pH goes above 7.0. **RULE OF THUMB:** check pH at least once a week - initially about two days after feeding and watering in.

At the risk of repetition, something more must be said about pH. pH is the mathematical scale of the hydrogen (acid) and hydroxyl (alkaline) ions. The pH scale goes from 0 to 14 and works like this: for every ten times you increase the concentration of the solution by either of the above elements, you change the pH scale by one number. Like 6 to 7 or 7 to 6. For more accurate pH detection use a short range indicator. This gives clearer colors than the long range indicator.

Fertilizers (Nutrients): There is no right formula. Every grower eventually develops his own for his own particular needs. Many growers use various applications of Peters, a fertilizer used mainly by florists throughout the industry. However for those who wish to mix their own fertilizer the following formulas are given:

7 3/4 ounces of Nitrate of soda.
2 ounces of Sulphate of potash
7 ounces of Superphosphate (16% phosphate)
2 1/2 ounces of Epsom Salts
1/4 ounce of Sulphate of Iron

This fertilizer should do well in most cases for the techniques proposed so far. Sand/gravel media are usually higher in pH than potted plant media. The medium used for potted plants is the same as that used for the bag technique which will be thoroughly discussed at the end of this section. If you are using commercial fertilizers, there will be ample trace elements already in the mixture. It is recommended you use the commercial mixes because they are much cheaper and do the job quite well. By commercial we mean those fifty pound bags you can buy at most rural feed stores. **Remember:** just a small pinch will do for potted plants. Here are 3 other mixtures in case you have trouble finding ingredients for the above.

Basic Mixture A:

12 1/2 ounces of Sodium nitrate
7 ounces of Superphosphate
4 ounces of Potassium sulphate
4 ounces of Magnesium sulphate
1/2 dram of Trace Elements

Basic Mixture B:

8 ounces of Ammonium sulphate
5 1/2 ounces of Ammonium phosphate
3 ounces of Muriate of potash
2 ounces of Calcium sulphate
1/2 dram of Trace Elements (as in A)

* You will notice trace elements were not given for the formula previous to A. Epsom salts and iron sulphate took care of that.

Basic Mixture C:

10 ounces of Ammonium sulphate
2 1/2 ounces of Potassium sulphate
6 ounces of Superphosphate
3 ounces of Magnesium sulphate
1/2 dram of Trace elements (as in A)

Buy the above at a feed store. Get the trace elements from a drugstore. You will need a scale to weigh these materials. Be especially careful in weighing the trace elements. A little goes a long way. The ratio by weight of the trace elements is: Zinc sulphate (3 parts), Boric acid (3 parts), Manganese sulphate (6 parts), Copper sulphate (1 part). The copper sulphate will prevent the formation of algae and fungus on the surface of your beds and pots. These separate parts total up to 13 parts. The simplest way to mix them would be by pounds. Even though a dram is very small, when you're fertilizing plants over a year, the drams will add up. Sixteen drams equals one ounce and 16 ounces equal one pound. So do it by thirteens. For example, thirteen pounds of trace element mixture would include 3 pounds of Zinc sulphate, 3 pounds of Boric acid, 6 pounds of Manganese sulphate, and 1 pound of Copper sulphate. You could do the same for ounces, for whatever you need.

Once again: most of us use Peters or some other pre-mixed commercial fertilizer. Here's a tip you can use: if you are using a small amount of fertilizer, mix it with sand so there will be an even amount of distribution upon the medium. For small packages of fertilizer you can contact Aero Engineering Corp, 2000 Calumet St, Clearwater, FL 33575. This company sells an 8-8-20 formula which is hydroponically balanced and is in one pound packages. Fertilizer formulas go like this: the first number (8) is for nitrogen, the second (8) is for Phosphate and the third (20) is for potash. Thus the mixture being sold here has 8 per cent nitrogen, 8 % phosphate and 20 % potash plus trace elements. This company sells at wholesale in case lots.

Eco Enterprises of 2821 NE 55th St, Seattle, WA 98105 has these plant fertilizer formulas:

10-8-14 - for house plants, flowers, tomatoes.
15-7-12 - for tropical foliage/flowers growing in a warm climate.
20-6-12 - for tropicals growing under tropical conditions.
3-35-10 - for tomatoes, cucumbers to promote root and flower production. Reduces leaf growth and is good in greenhouses with low roofs. Of course you can find similar formulations at other companies.

Some facts to know:

Plants use more potassium on cloudy days. Dull weather over several days will just about double the requirement. Potassium nitrate an be used for potassium. Calcium nitrate can be used in conjunction with potassium nitrate in order to supply the necessary nitrogen and eliminate sodium. Use the granular form for both chemicals. In all your mixtures it's a good idea to add the sulphate of iron last because it evaporates and loses its potency rather quickly. The entire mixture should be applied immediately to the areas concerned.

Foliage requires a higher rate of nitrogen than blooming or fruiting plants. Some growers use Rapid Gro (25-19-17). Flowering plants do well on phosphate fertilizers (5-10-5 for example). In order to develop more rigid stems during periods of dark weather, use more potash. A formula such as 16-18-24 will do the trick. Keep in mind that as plants feed the pH gradually changes toward alkalinity. The nitrate and phosphate are more quickly removed from nutrient solutions than the potassium and calcium. Adjust your feeding accordingly. Plants can have an iron deficiency even though there is iron in their tissues. The iron reacts with the phosphates inside the plant, causing the iron to become unavailable to the chlorophyll molecule in the plant. A saturated bed or pot will cause an iron deficiency. When this happens, lightly spray the surface of the medium with a 1% solution of iron sulphate (10 ounces to 5 pints of water). The medium should be moist before spraying.

Since there is less light in winter, apply less fertilizer during winter months. Keep in mind that aeration is more important than nutrition. If a plant's growth is slow but everything else seems okay, you probably have an aeration problem. Sometimes just a slight raking of the medium surface will help. The roots of the plant will feed more rapidly from a dilute solution provided you have ample aeration. Nitrogen is absorbed faster than the other elements so you must adjust your solution or mixture accordingly. If the superphosphate is not supplying enough calcium, add a little calcium nitrate. Finally, keep all your mixes, fertilizers and trace elements in tightly sealed containers and stored in a dry area such as the potting shed.

Nutrient toxicity, deficiency:

Trace elements are hardly ever deficient, especially if you use commercial fertilizers or mix from one of the basic formulas. It's almost impossible to diagnose for deficiencies. But there excess is quite toxic. So be careful. You should be on the lookout for deficiencies and toxicity for all the elements. **RULE OF THUMB FOR AVOIDING TOXICITY:** flush the entire system with water only after every third feeding. Some media come pre-mixed with nutrient, so check with your supplier. You have to be on the alert for toxicity.

Watch the pH of your system! Do not try to get an accurate measurement of pH with litmus paper. Litmus is only for rough estimates. Use a good pH kit instead. Healthy plants will take what they need from a solution if the pH is within the proper range. Most vegetables like a pH of 6.2 to 6.8. Also check the salinity (salt residue) of the solution or medium with an electrical conductivity meter (E.C. meter). This will tell you the ion balance or imbalance within the solution or media. In other words pH testing should also include the media.

Plants change the nutrient solution as soon as they begin taking up nutrient. If you are using the bag technique, your worries are limited because the solution should always be the same and you will leach with water after every third feeding. Thus you will get rid of salt accumulation. If you are using other techniques? Keep an ample volume of solution, make a constant check on composition, and disorders will be less likely to occur. Successful growers can give a rough diagnosis of their crops at any given time. They can tell if anything is wrong. The more experience you have, the more accurately you can make a diagnosis.

Though inadequate when compared to laboratory testing, quick tests can be made with the HACH Chemical Company plant analysis kit (P O Box 389, Loveland, CO 80539). Since laboratory analysis can be slow, there are faster ways to respond to a problem. Hydroponics lends itself nicely to this procedure. If you think you've diagnosed the problem, isolate a few plants and double or triple the amount of the element in question and see what happens the next few days. In any case don't be too quick to jump to conclusions. Don't over-react. You could add an extra feeding to your regular number of feedings - within the given time schedule. Do nothing else until you're sure this has corrected the problem. Even then, when you have to do something, do not increase the nutrient solution's strength by more than 20%. One last tip: usually healthy new growth on a plant does not indicate a nutrient deficiency.

Towards a more detailed analysis:

As stated before, bag culture normally will not have these symptoms if you irrigate with plain water at regular intervals. No matter what technique your using, if you have larger volumes of nutrient in solution you'll be more able to control toxicity or deficiency. If you formulate for the plant in question you should be able to avoid most problems.

When it comes to trace elements, the following concentrations are considered to be toxic. Using tomatoes as an example with ppm per dry weight as the basis: more than 150 ppm of Boron, more than 500 ppm of Manganese, more than 300 ppm of Zinc. For cucumbers: more than 200 ppm of Boron, more than 550 ppm of Manganese, more than 650 ppm of Zinc. For lettuce: more than 300 ppm of Boron, more than 250 ppm of Manganese, more than 350 ppm of Zinc. Excesses normally occur with copper, boron, manganese, nitrogen, phosphorous and salts which include chloride. Those who work with hydroponics can normally expect excesses and deficiencies in all major and some minor elements. That's why the smart grower makes regular checks on his nutrient mix and solution as well as having dry plant samples analyzed at laboratories. Weekly, sometimes daily, checks on nutrient solutions are needed for top production.

To repeat: plants are constantly taking up nutrient from the feeding solution. This in itself will give rise to both deficiencies and excesses. That's why the nutrient solution must be checked and replenished when necessary. But even though a deficiency or excess can show up dramatically so also can it diminish rapidly if corrections are promptly made.

You must control the medium and you have to accurately analyze what's going on. And like with disease symptoms, you have to be sure it's not insect damage you are looking at. Normally a plant's growth will be considerably slowed before the symptoms appear. Old leaves show first any problems which indicate nitrogen, phosphorous or potassium. While young leaves at their growing points show what's going on with boron, zinc, manganese, copper, iron and calcium. There are four areas to watch. These are: the root system, the shoot or growing point, old leaves, new leaves. Roots can show the following: toxic copper which causes browning, aluminum which causes stunting. The principal plant symptoms are stunting, chlorosis (yellowing), tissue death or local necrosis, and purpling.

Sometimes a grower is too busy to wait for a long drawn-out analysis from a distant laboratory. He can do some things for himself by running tests on the plant in question. He can ask the following questions and perform the necessary adjustments.

1. Does this plant have a deficiency of nutrients? How about toxicity?

A.   See if the plant improves if you make a change. You could either double or halve the nutrient supply or you could boost up or retard the rate of flow.

2. Which nutrient is causing the trouble?

A.   Do the same as the above with the suspected nutrient only. With micro-nutrients such as Boron you could use a foliar spray to see if you get improvement for a suspected deficiency.

3. Is the pH out of whack? Or is there too much salt?

A.   In the first case use a pH meter which is correctly calibrated. In the second case use an Electrical Conductivity meter.

4. Is it the water?

A.   Have your water analyzed from time to time. Water also can change in content.

CHART OF NUTRIENT SYMPTOMS

NUTRIENT	TOXIC	DEFICIENT
Nitrogen	Foliage lush, thick. Poor fruiting. Stems and stalk elongated.	Older leaves turn yellow. Slow growth. Deeply colored fruit. Plant turns pale.
Calcium	Rare but looks like magnesium or potassium deficiency.	Fruit gets "blossom end rot". Leaf margins yellow, turn brown. Younger leaves stop growing. Stunted roots, shoots.
Magnesium	Poor growth. Shows up as calcium or potassium deficinecy.	Plant turns green, but older leaf margins turn yellow - then leaf sections turn brown. New leaves pale, die.
Phosphorus	Shows up as zinc deficiency. Plants grow slowly.	Mottled edges - red areas. Plant is first dark green, then "purples" in older and young veins. Plant pales, stops growing.
Potassium	Shows up as a calcium or magnesium deficiency.	Like phosphorous but leaves become scorched. Dead and dying spots occur on leaves and margins.
Zinc	Yellow plants, stunted. Shows up as iron or manganese deficiency.	New leaves are twisted, stunted, necrotic, rosette, perhaps yellow. Sometimes grayish.
Iron	Rarely occurs under normal conditions.	General yellowing in newest leaves. Veins last to turn yellow.
Molybdenum	Rarely occurs.	Plant is green but has inter-veinal yellowing. New leaves turn white, have drying edges. Old leaf margins curl, roll.
Sulphur	Rarely occurs.	Similar to nitrogen deficiency but more general.
Copper	Stunted growth and death. Roots stunted, browning.	Leaves yellow; curled margins. Young shoots die; no more fruiting. Plant is pale green.

NUTRIENT	TOXIC	DEFICIENT
Boron	Stunted growth and death.	Growing tips die. Rough, cracked stems with ridges, spots. Poor fruit set. Dies back.
Manganese	Necrotic spots, stunted plants with deficiencies which look like iron or zinc.	Young leaves yellow with green veins. Spots, streaks on the leaves and black specks on the stems. Similar to iron deficiency.
Chlorine	Rarely occurs. Plants wilt, stunt. Old leaves have dead spots.	Rarely occurs. Old leaves turn to bronze then yellow.
Aluminum	Roots stunted.	

Some further tips:

- AMMONIUM FERTILIZER: Don't use on floral crops in the winter.
- One authority recommends you use phosphoric acid to lower pH and potassium bicarbonate to raise it.
- When using extra lighting for tomatoes, don't go beyond 18 hours a day because tomatoes need a dark period to do well.

Problems not related to nutrient toxicity, deficiency:

When a plant is in trouble:

First check the following: too cold, too hot, dirty leaves, animal or insect pests, poor ventilation, nutrient solution too strong or too weak, medium too dry or too wet, not enough nutrient solution in tank (or not enough fertilizer in bed or pot). Also, maybe too much light, too little light, water dripping on the plants.

Healthy but yellow leaves: pH out of range for plant's use.

Leaves yellow and then fall: too cold, too dry, too much water.

Healthy leaves suddenly drop: too cold, too dry, too much water, shock from sudden changes such as temperature or light.

Wilting: too hot, too dry, too much water.

Variegated leaves don't variegate: not enough light.

Leaves have brown spots, margins: too much water, too much nutrient, too hot, too dry, too much sun or light.

Leaves and stems rot: too much water, too much humidity, fungus or disease infection.

Plants grow poorly: too much water, too cold, not enough nutrient.

Flowers, buds drop: too much water, too dry, too cold, sudden changes of temperature or light.

Notice how many times overwatering occurs? Amateurs as well as professionals have a tendency to overwater. A rule of thumb is to push your index finger as far down as it will go into the medium. If you feel any moisture at all then the plant does not need any water.

Also you can use a meter or sensoring device. Just remember more plants are killed by overwatering than by anything else. Too dry or too cold means the air surrounding the plant. There are other things which can go wrong - just like in any other business. Good housekeeping is essential. The growing area should be fenced off to keep out stray animals. Keep the weeds and grass mowed around the entire area. Keep the shed and greenhouse neat and clean. Keep all pathways clean. Don't allow loose materials to lie around where bugs and mice might hide. When applicable, keep the plants open to the air and pollination from bees.

To repeat: don't allow moisture to drip from overhead and onto the plants. Make sure you have good ventilation. Sow all seeds and cuttings at the same time.

Don't set up a hydroponicum where trees will shut out the sun. But trees are useful for a windbreak. If you have them, then build near them. Try not to build your hydroponicum in a polluted area. Keep the birds out. If you start out right, most of the above will hardly ever occur. Plants, like humans, are difficult to kill. You require almost a direct hit to do the job. In order to kill a plant with kindness, you would have to pour the fertilizer, undiluted, directly upon it.

In a large measure our world depends for its survival on more and more people "farming" the hydroponic way. The methods proposed in this book do take a little manual labor in getting started, particularly if you start out with the sand/gravel technique as described in this section. But afterwards, when you are more experienced, pumps and electricity will do the hard work for you. When you do decide to go commercial as described in Section Two, you will in a short time hire others to do the potting, planting, harvesting and packaging. Even that cannot be classified as hard work. If you've ever done intensive gardening the organic way, you'd know what hard work is!

In Blooming Prairie, MN, a grower uses an NFT system developed by and purchased from an outfit in Ohio. The system is familiar to our readers: it features the NFT trough with plastic cap to keep out the light and with holes at regular intervals for seedling plug-in.

What makes this grower's system unique is that he is doing it in Minnesota! We receive letters every day from people who think the winters are too severe even as far north as St. Louis. You only have to look around just about anywhere in the United States and Canada to find an on-going hydroponic operation working full-steam ahead.

Marketing in the grower's area? He finds the market exceeding his expectations. His best marketing technique is this: when he gets a customer he keeps him by furnishing quality and consistency of product. His best customers are area hospitals, some supermarkets and an occasional produce warehouse.

The grower grows Bibb lettuce and some leaf lettuce. He intends to stay with two or three crops instead of too many. This feeling comes from his background in farming where he found it more efficient to concentrate his efforts on two or three crops rather than to spread himself too thinly.

CHAPTER 4

SOME FURTHER NECESSARY INFORMATION

Plans of action: Let's discuss the different ways you could choose to go into hydroponics.

Plan A. This is for those who want to start out slow or have a full-time job and want to putter around before getting at it. If you like vegetables, start up a couple of sand/gravel beds. If you'd rather work with potted plants, then set up a table or two.

Plan B. You're serious. You want to get at it. But you see more profit potential in potted plants. So set up all your houses specifically for this. Start out with two or three houses and keep building. There is much more profit than $40,000 with 1/3 acre of potted plants. Especially with tropicals and other foliage.

Plan C. You're serious also. But you see where the future demands more growers of vegetables and grains. You can earn a good living with vegetables. If you also grow some sword-fern baskets you'll realize that extra profit which will enable you to get along that much faster. Don't forget herbs - this will be a large market someday.

Plan D. According to one large grower, there is a lot of money to be made in growing annuals for the spring and summer trade.

Plan E. You're over sixty and tired of the shovel, the tiller, the compost. Then by all means throw together two sand/gravel beds and grow all the food you can eat - with a lot less work after the initial installation. Put up a table or two and have some flowering plants year-round. It'll make life more meaningful.

Some ideas on what to plant and when:

Early spring for sand/gravel beds.
For Northern states, plant leeks as twice as close as in soil, horseradish (if you can find an economic source - use heavy crown only), cantaloupe, honeydew melon, chile peppers. Not all of them - just two or three crops to fill your beds. The chile pepper market is a very large one and you might consider getting into it. Southern states will plant any or all of the above except that leeks should be planted in the fall to go through winter and be harvested in the spring. Again, plant everything just far enough apart so their leaves will barely touch when the plants are mature. For both North and South (or East and West), be sure to plant fern. Don't forget. Good 12 inch specimen fern fetch very good prices. Fern likes semi-shade and moisture.

Early spring for potted plants:

Start up with African violets for summer and early fall sales. Also mums, ivies, pothos, croton in all states. Other plants to consider are ficus, peperomia, sanseveria, begonia, philedendron, aloe vera. If you develop your markets for African violets you can make a very good living from that item alone.

Late summer for sand/gravel beds:

You might call this "getting ready for winter." For both Northern and Southern states plant Brussel sprouts, cauliflower, bibb lettuce, and broccoli. These crops will go into the first weeks of hard winter inside the plastic house we suggested. They will be harvested by then because you can plant them earlier in the North than in the South. The lettuce sells as fast as it matures.

Late summer for potted areas:

Get ready to sell all of your mums and African violets. In late fall, plant pots and trays of daffodil, hyacinth, narcissus, calla lily, tulip - to be sold in January and February. Some of these plants need a dormancy period in low temperature - so follow the planting instructions for each. Also start gloxinia for sale at Christmas and in January. Start amaryllis for the same reason.

These are just a few of the many things you can do. Of course when you erect a commercial greenhouse (as described in Section Two) all of this will change. Some other ideas: Chinese vegetables like bok choy are quite popular around the major cities. Make money here by catering to Chinese and Vietnamese stores and restaurants. Assure them high quality produce and you will have a good market. Although there will be some more growing tips for plants, you should still do yourself a favor. Go to the library and get up-to-date texts on the plants you want to grow. Mums, gloxinia, African violets, begonia, cyclamen and hydrangea need more detailed knowledge than we can include here.

Always remember that this is a business. As such we want to gain the highest profit possible. Attention to detail separates the winners from the also-rans. You must remain alert. A good grower doesn't let a day go by when he isn't checking his plants, seeing how they are doing. A top-notch hydroponist keeps accurate records and is in his hydroponicum every day.

When does the plastic go up?

As soon as possible. As soon as you can afford it. You don't want heavy rains in the beds or the pots. You'll want to avoid late spring frosts. In the South, you'll want to get ready for summer and place plastic shading over the houses. Some crops like sun, some don't. Be smart - don't force the plants to do it your way. High winds, heavy (sometimes acid) rains, hot sun - be prepared to avoid them. In a word the plastic goes up early and stays there. If your pocket is thin, you'll have to devise ways to overcome those obstacles which get in your way. This book shows you how to begin, but your goal is to lengthen your growing season as soon as possible. **That's where the money is!** For some plants it will be better to use wood lath for shading. This can be expensive unless you can find an inexpensive source or get the wood free.

Why not place these plants in the shade of your house, or the shed? Or under trees? Improvise! Make-do! This section gives you the basic start-up, but Section Two gives you all the specifics for a sophisticated commercial operation.

Some growing directions:

   Chrysanthemums: Why? Because they are a crop which makes consistent profit at almost any time of the year but mostly in the fall and early winter. If you're going to make your own cuttings instead of buying starter plants elsewhere, the following directions will help. For propagation, take cuttings from selected stock. The cuttings should not be soft or woody. Place them in a rooting medium (vermiculite) after using a rooting hormone. Do this early in the year when temperatures are around 45 degrees. Cuttings should be rooted in small 3 inch pots - for mums. If this is an extra expense for you then root in the vermiculite and transfer to a six inch pot. Place three or four of these rooted cuttings in each six inch pot. Place the cuttings under a plastic "tent". Do not allow moisture to accumulate on the inside roof of the tent. After the cuttings are well-rooted, keep moist with a nutrient solution. In late spring transfer to the tables after all danger of frost has passed.

   Stopping the plant. This is nipping the terminal bud so that side shoots will form. This should not be done until the plant begins to break or bud. Only the small tip of the growing point is taken out. Then allow the plant to break (bud) naturally. Stop a second time in mid-summer, after the first breaks are producing side shoots. Remove the growing point. Reduce phosphate by one half after flower buds appear.

Tuberous-rooted begonias:

   These are grown from tubers instead of seed. Early in the spring, bury the tubers in a box of damp peat moss and keep the temperature at sixty degrees. When the roots have started and stem buds start appearing, pot with 25% peat moss and 75% sand. Feed sparingly until the plants are well rooted. After potting reduce the temperature slightly. Place the pots inside a "house" and shade from bright sunny days.

   African violets: These are started by rooting their leaves in a moist medium. Moisture should be added from time to time, but do not let the moisture touch the leaves. When rooted, pot in a 50-50 mixture of peat moss and sand. African violets are usually potted in four inch pots. When feeding, always keep the moisture away from the crown and the leaves. There is a vast library devoted to African violets and their culture. To become adept at growing this plant, you definitely must acquaint yourself with the literature.

   Hyacinths: These must undergo several weeks of refrigeration to get them started, especially in the South. Daffodils and narcissus are also easy to grow and must be treated the same way. They all grow well in sand/gravel culture, even in gravel alone. If you plant them in "dressy" plates or trays, you will get a higher price for them. After they have had their cooling off period (check Chapter 11 and planting directions at supplier), plant them in the medium you have chosen and keep the medium moist but not wet.

Hydrangeas: Good money-makers, but their culture is a little more complicated. A discussion of hydrangeas is better left to a standard text on the subject. Especially on how to get the different colors and what fertilizers to use. (The aim here is to give you hints, possibilities. These plants by no means cover the entire field of possibilities. After you have done the marketing for your area, your choice of plants may widely differ from those offered in this book. It's what the customer wants which counts.)

INSECT CONTROL:

Even the cleanest among us has bugs now and then. But basically if you keep a clean house, destroy crop residue, use clean media, sterilize everything inside the greenhouse between crops, keep weeds out and cut down around the outside for a reasonable distance, don't bring in infested plants, you should start off with no insects.

However, with today's intensified production it's sometimes difficult to maintain all of the above desirable activities. Some insects will find you out by just riding in on the wind. You can't keep the greenhouse tight all of the time. So you'll need to know how to identify insects early on before they get a head start. You can't expect insecticides or biological controls to do the whole job for you. You will still have to maintain good housekeeping. And you'll need to know under what conditions certain insects are likely to appear and at what times of the year. If you don't know bugs you will have to learn. Those you find and don't know must be quickly identified by an expert. Extension agents and local universities will be happy to help you identify unfamiliar species. They can also suggest corrective measures. Relying heavily upon insecticides is self-defeating because the government is taking more and more of these insecticides off the market or is placing more of them under tighter control. Most growers are moving away from the use of insecticides and are looking toward more rewarding techniques.

For example, a lot of insects which are harmful to your crops are attracted to the color yellow. Many commercial growers now hang up long strips of sticky yellow tape. These strips are 6-8 inches wide and hang all the way from the rafters to the floor. They are hung at least ten feet apart. It has been estimated that these yellow bands will reduce each generation of whiteflies by 50%. Not to mention what they do to cut down on leafminers, thrips, gnats, aphids and fungus gnats, all of which are among the worst predators of your crops. Like anything else which will do an effective job, these yellow bands must be up before you start your crop.

Other methods include setting up a greenhouse environment which is not favorable to certain insects. Misting to delay the spread of spider mites is a good example. When coupled with the introduction of predatory mites which feed on the spider mites the mist will keep the spider mites down low enough on the plant so the predatory mites can get to them. European growers have had great success with predatory insects intent on devouring their crops. The secret is to introduce the predatory insects at the first sign of insect infestation. This means you have to make daily inspections to determine if you have an infestation. You and your workers should be trained to look for both plant damage and insects. The sooner the problem is found the better.

Misting must be done early in the day to avoid other adverse conditions to plant growth. To date, misting seems to reduce both spider mite and whitefly populations. A predatory fungus (Cephalosporium lecanii) has been used for years to control whitefly populations. But this fungus requires high humidity to do its job. With regular misting this fungus can easily spread and control whitefly. But there is a limit to how much misting you should do. Too much water introduces pathogens and limits your efforts toward eliminating the whitefly. A reduced but regular schedule for misting seems to be in order. Good air circulation is mandatory during and after misting. An added advantage of misting is that all the water falls to the floor where, if you have previously placed your plants on plastic where thrips and leafminers pupate, you can succeed in drowning them. But again, be careful in misting - too much is to much.

You must come to a point where you can accept some level of insect damage. With vegetables that's not much of a problem because the fruit is what you're normally selling. However when it comes to ornamentals and flowering plants, unless you're selling cut flowers and seed, you have an entirely different problem. In this case you can't allow much damage to be done. So have your control program set up and in action before an infestation occurs. Know how to accurately identify insects from their appearance and from the damage they cause. If you're using biological control, keep the growing area or greenhouse closed between crops in order to keep any predatory insects inside for the next crop. And consider cultivars which are more resistant to insects.

Insect detection and control: Specific insects:

Leafminers:

Type of damage: L. Trifolii, the so-called American Leafminer, can cause tremendous damage. The adult or egg-laying variety is a small black fly which has yellow markings. The female makes stings or holes in a vein on the upper side of the leaf. She lays her eggs in this sting. Such visible stings are the first sign of infestation. The eggs hatch into larvae which feed and tunnel through the leaf until they are ready to mature at which time they drop to the ground and pupate.

Control: Cleanliness is of the utmost importance. This means an interruption of crops or crop rotation and thorough clean up of all crop residues. Crop interruption will prevent high infestations from occurring. Parasitic control is diglyphus spp or dacnusa spa. Leafminers are very adaptive to insecticides. Present effective insecticides are: triazophos, avermectin, pyrazophos, chlorpyrifos with avermectin.

Whitefiles:

Type of damage: The young secrete a honeydew which is soon covered by a black fungus which can easily be seen. Also the adult fly can be seen rising from the plant when you brush the leaves with your hand. The fungus will soon kill the plant, not to mention the deleterious effect it has on the plant's appearance. The black fungus is the more serious type of damage, but the young can also damage the plant through their feeding cycle. Some other symptoms caused but not restricted to the whitefly are: new growth becomes curled and yellow, leaves appear yellow and speckled.

Control: At the first sign of whiteflies, growers in Europe introduce a parasitic wasp (Encarsia formosa) which deposits eggs in the whitefly nymphs. The eggs will hatch and devour the nymphs. These wasp larvae can keep the whitefly population at a low level. Whiteflies are very adaptive to insecticides. Some present insecticides which work are systemics like butocarboxim and aldicarb. Because whitefly in its various growth stages can at times be immune to non-systemics, these insecticides must be applied every 5-6 days in order to reduce the whitefly population. Pyrethoids are good for this. The effective ones are: fenpropathrin, permethrin and cypermethrin.

Aphids:

Type of damage: Aphids cause a sooty residue on the plant's surface. Their presence also detracts from the plant's appearance. Other damage can be (like whitefly) new growth which is yellow or speckled leaves.

Control: This is another insect which readily adapts to insecticides. But since a lot of growers are moving toward biological control, a new tiny fly has come on the market which lays eggs near the aphid. The eggs develop into small orange larvae which devour aphids with great gusto. More importantly the little flies can multiply indefinitely as long as there are aphids about. They become welcome and permanent guests within the greenhouse. The name of this predatory fly is aphid midge or Aphidoletes aphidimyza. You can get them from: Troy Hygrow Systems, 4096 Highway East, East Troy, WI 53120; Applied Pest control, PO Box 2637, Sidney, BC V8L-4C1, Canada; Organic Pest Control, Box 55267, Seattle, WA 98155. You must get an importation permit from USDA, APHIS, PP&Q, Federal Center Building, Hyattsville, MD 20872 (Form 526). "Ladybugs" are also a good control.

Mites:

Type of damage: New growth curled, sometimes yellow and distorted. The leaves and stems are speckled yellow and may have webbing. These symptoms are visible on top of the leaves, but it's better to make periodic checks under the leaves to be sure. Why? Because mites, especially spider mites, are the number one pest in greenhouses! They are particularly bad on foliage plants such as schefflera and croton. They love Areca palms. You almost need a magnifying glass to see them. These mites sometimes attack tomatoes and cucumbers where the leaves and tops (petioles) of the plants can be killed. These symptoms are sometimes mistaken for magnesium deficiency or too much manganese.

Control: If you have a heavy infestation (the webbing is thick) it will be difficult to get the insecticide through the webbing and onto the insects. Therefor non-systemic insecticides must be used at least twice at a 5-7 day interval. You have to detect these creatures as early as possible in order to keep the upper hand. Mites are quite adaptable. What works one time on them may be an appetizer to them the next time. So you have to change your treatment methods and patterns as well as insecticides. Chemicals used for control are: hexahis, kelthane, dicofol and dienochlor. But we like to stay with the pyrethoids if at all possible. Two of these are fenpropathrin and fluvalinate. Try to keep the temperature down in the greenhouse. These insects, as well as most insects, thrive at high temperatures. When you keep the temperature down you can use biological control such as Phytosieulus persimillis, a predatory mite. It's essential to introduce these predatory mites as soon as possible - before the spider mites become a large infestation. Also green lacewings are effective.

Fungus gnats:

Type of damage: These are also known as Sciarid Flies. They apparently cause little damage unless a plant is young when the larvae can feed on the root system. The adults look like small grey-winged flies. The main objection to them is that they are a nuisance in a retail situation and may cause customer disapproval.

Control: Best to attack the larvae with a drenching spray of either resmethrin, oxaml or bendiocarb. The adults can be controlled with most aerosol fumigants. It has been suggested that these insects like conditions where algae and pathogens thrive. Rockwool is known to promote both of these conditions. Again, sanitation takes precedence in insect as well as disease control.

Thrips:

Type of damage: The leaves appear to have thin "windows" which also appear as streaks or specks. These symptoms occur because the insects eat away the green plant tissue and leave the rib-like structure untouched. Low humidity and warm temperature give an ideal climate for thrips. Many of them are carried into the greenhouse or growing area from plants obtained elsewhere. Some species can winter over in wheat and barley fields and then enter the greenhouse in early summer. The most prevalent thrip is known as Onion Thrips.

Control: When thrips do appear they do so in large numbers, usually from a nearby field. You will have to be aware of their imminent approach throughout the growing season. They can also winter over inside the greenhouse so it's best to stagger or skip crops in order to deter any suspect thrip population. Methods used besides chemical control are:beating leaves above a sheet of paper in order to expose the bugs, watch for damage symptoms, and use of yellow sticky tapes and traps. Chemical methods which can be used are a pyrethroid coupled with polybutene applied to plastic on the floor below the plant. The thrips drop to the plastic, get stuck by the polybutene and become exposed to the pyrethroid. Other chemicals used are endosulfan, bendiocarb, dimethoate and chlorpyrifos. Biological control for thrips is amblysens cucumeris.

Worms or Caterpillars:

Type of damage: Presence of these insects can be seen by the bits of fecal matter which drop to the leaves below. This waste is usually black and in pellet form. Cabbage Loopers are famous for this. Other worms and larvae will turn a plant into a skeleton by stripping leaves as well as stems. They can decimate a lettuce patch overnight. Other worms such as leafrollers will roll up a leaf around them. The list of worms is endless.

Control: When at all possible, it's best to use biological control on any insect infestation. Your best chances are to catch the infestation before it gets too far along. Bacillus thuringiensis is a well known biological control which works with most caterpillars which chew on plants. One species of wasp, Trichogramma, is also used. Chemical controls are the pyrethroids, methamidophos, acephate and methomyl. Each worm has its own defenses - so each needs specific attention. After you have identified the species in question, can find out which control method is best.

Scale:
Type of damage: This insect exudes a honeydew which later turns into black soot. The leaves of the host plant soon become yellow. There will be circular yellow spots on the upper surface of the leaves. Beneath these spots will be raised mounds which are the insects surrounded by hard shells from which the insect gets its name. Once the insect is imbedded inside this shell the only way it can be destroyed is with a systemic insecticide because the insect is feeding on the sap of the plant. Contact insecticides are only effective while the insect is crawling about.

A Word of Caution: The above brief discussion doesn't come any where near to covering all insects which can cause damage to your crops. But the most important and most harmful are the ones just discussed. Be careful with insecticides. Whenever possible try to find a biological control or use natural insecticides obtained from pyrethrins and rotenone. Especially is this important for vegetable crops. Insecticides used to stop foliar damage must be handled with care. The EPA is getting more strict about how insecticides should be handled. Employees and other users of insecticides must be protected at all times. Preferably no one should be allowed to go back into an area where insecticide has been applied for at least 24 hours after application. **NEVER USE SYSTEMIC INSECTICIDES ON VEGETABLES!**

While we're at it, here's some control tips for tomatoes, lettuce and cucumber:

For whitefly: use a pyrethrum derivative such as pyrethoid.
For spider mites: use kelthane or mild soapy water.
For aphids: use pyrethoid or rotenone. Spray in the evening after the cooling system has been shut off. Use a high pressure sprayer which gives out a fine mist. Spray again two days later and on the third day. Wait a week, spray again. Repeat four days in a row. Spray every 2-4 days after that. Vary chemical spray content.

DISEASE CONTROL:
Carelessness opens the door to big losses. Have you ever smoked in the greenhouse? You better not. Not unless you want to have your tomato plants infected by the tobacco mosaic virus! Even if you smoke outside the growing area or the greenhouse and don't thoroughly wash

38

your hands before going back to work, you'll still spread the virus. Many a grower has wiped out entire crops this way!

Knowing there are pitfalls let's consider the conditions favorable for disease. Temperature and moisture are the prime factors. Temperatures too high or too low will be damaging. Too much water will cause some diseases to start, notably root rot. Improper ventilation and defective heaters can add to the situation. Overcrowding of plants isn't good either. (Pathogens is the term given to these disease invaders: bacterium, fungus, mycoplasm, virus.) For example, if the temperature range from day to night is wide, your greenhouse atmosphere could end up with 100% humidity at night! This is the same thing as watering down the leaves. What happens then? Pathogen activity rises and you may be faced with some foliar damage.

Disease results when three factors are present. First there must be a favorable environment. Second a viable pathogen must be present. And third there must be a susceptible plant, one which genetically cannot resist invasion. If any one of these three is absent disease cannot occur. **DIAGNOSIS OF THE DISEASE IS OF PARAMOUNT IMPORTANCE!** Don't assume a symptom on a plant is caused by a disease. It could be an insect infestation. Or a nutrient problem, An accurate diagnosis is needed. Most of you will in time learn the symptoms of the various diseases. Meanwhile if you don't know don't be afraid to ask your nearest university or county extension agent. That's what they're there for.

So what do you do?

The environment inside the growing area should consist of the following. Particularly for foliage and flowering plants, all plants should be off the floor - preferably on benches or tables. In the beginning, you may have the pots sitting on top of plastic which lies on the ground. This is all right for a start, but get to the tables as soon as possible. Also sufficient light for the species being grown should be provided. Watering must be done in such a way which minimizes getting leaves or foliage excessively wet, especially toward evening. The water used must be pathogen free.

You must start with healthy plants, preferably those cultivars which are disease resistant. These plants must be pathogen free and you should deal only with those stock providers who can furnish such plants. Propagation must be conducted in media which is pathogen free. Some peat providers may be getting peat from cultivated shallow bogs wherein pathogens reign wildly. If in doubt about your peat source, you should have it steam pasteurized before using it. Always use fresh peat when you propagate new plants. If you have to use unsterilized peat for foliage and ornamentals, then it's best to rotate one species from another. Some plants which are susceptible to unsterilized peat are: Peperomia, Dieffenbachia, Schefflera, Pothos, Neanthe bella palm, tomatoes, cucumbers and melons. **DO NOT USE AMMONIUM SOURCES OF NITROGEN IN STERILIZED PEAT!** All pots and tools should be thoroughly clean. Transporting plants form one area to another must be done with care. Damage brought about from rough handling can only make matters worse. Other sensible factors would include: media which drains good and contains plenty of air pockets, pots placed on surfaces which drain fast, and watering with care.

When looking at symptoms examine all the facts before making a decision. A lot of diseases can be avoided if you know your crop and what cultivation it requires. If something's wrong perhaps you have the wrong growing conditions for that particular crop. Often a magnifying glass will bring to light the problem - like mites, insects, fungi spores. Suppose you've made a correct diagnosis. You've found your crop does have a disease. It doesn't have an insect infestation nor are environmental conditions unfavorable.

What do you do now?

First ask yourself if anything can be done now or should you wait and use preventative measures for the next crop? Are just a few plants involved? Will the disease spread? If not, throw those few plants outside and burn them. Did you find a virus infection? You'll probably not be able to save the plant - the disease is systemic (it's inside the plant). Do you think spraying will be worthwhile? If the plant is heavily infected, spraying won't do much good. Diseases must be caught in their early stages of development for you to gain effective control. How about equipment? Do you have the proper kind to do the job? Diseases do re-occur. Be prepared for them in the future. Some pathogens can last for years in a hydroponic system. Ultra violet lamps can help a lot in getting rid of pathogens in the nutrient solution. But suppose you have more than one disease with which to cope? Treat the one which demands immediate attention, like damping off of seedlings.

Vegetables are the easiest for disease control. Tropicals and foliage have a long list of pathogens. Too long to go into in this book. Your best bet if you're interested in growing these plants is to get a text which specializes in foliar production. One of the best texts for this is Joiner's **FOLIAGE PLANT PRODUCTION** which is listed at the end of this book.

Some vegetable diseases and their control:

TOMATOES HAVE THE FOLLOWING DISEASES: Fusarium wilt and Verticillium wilt, leaf spot and early blight, tobacco mosaic virus, Botrytis or gray mold, and leaf mold. In the wilt category, plants with this will wilt easily on hot days. Soon they wilt all the time and the leaves turn yellow. Cutting the plant right above the surface of the soil will expose a dark ring just under the outer layers of green cells. There is no cure for a plant thus infected. Control can be achieved by sterilizing the medium.

Leaf spot and early blight give the following symptoms: spots on the leaves. Early blight gives you dark looking rings against a background of brown. Leaf spot shows black dots in the infected area. The older leaves are infected first. Soon they fall from the plant. So reduce relative humidity and install better ventilation even if you have to remove some of the plant's lower leaves.

Tobacco mosaic virus distorts the leaves. The plants are stunted and will not produce. No smoking in the growing area is the order of the day. All workers must wash their hands before going into the growing area. Insect prevention must be maintained because insects, especially the sucking variety, will sometimes carry the disease.

Botrytis or gray mold is a fungus infection. It will grow along with the plant and when it encircles a stem the plant will die. Get rid of all infected plants - preferably by burning them at a distance outside. Good ventilation is necessary as well as lowering the relative humidity. Sometimes in the early stage of infection the fungicide Ferbam can be pasted over the infected area which has been previously scraped clean.

Small gray spots on the underside of the leaf will sometimes spread and cause a pale area to appear on the upper surface of the leaf. This is leaf spot. Soon other spots will appear. Again good ventilation and sanitation are needed as well as lowering the humidity. In the initial phase fungicides can reduce losses.

CUCUMBERS HAVE THE FOLLOWING DISEASES: Fusarium wilt, Botrytis, powdery mildew, and mosaic virus (cucumber or CMV). For Botrytis and wilt follow the procedures outlined for tomatoes. CMV causes infected leaves to be dwarf-like and thin. Only good sanitation can prevent this disease from getting started and going further. Powdery mildew looks like particles of snow on the top layer of the leaf. The infection spreads rapidly and gets larger in size. Best control: adequate ventilation and sanitation. Some chemical control can help.

MAIN CONCERN FOR NFT SYSTEMS: Pythium wilt causes root rot in NFT systems. Being a water mold which can swim, Pythium wilt can quickly infect any hydroponic system which relies on a constant nutrient flow. The symptoms are: small roots become mushy and soft. Larger roots are brown and tan. By this time the process is irreversible and the plant dies. Control is difficult. Avoid all soil particles. Hands, fingernails, shoes, clothes - all must be thoroughly clean. Be careful in the transplants you use. Sometimes the water source can carry the problem.

CHAPTER 5

MARKETING: What it's all about.

Without a market you are nowhere. **NEVER START GROWING ANYTHING UNTIL YOU HAVE ESTABLISHED A MARKET FOR IT.** Not having a market can break you. Obvious, right? You'd be surprised at the number of people who won't heed this advice and have learned the hard way what needs to be done. That's why this book has a lot of space devoted to marketing. To start you don't just run out and begin "bargaining". How are you going to bargain when you don't yet know how to grow at a profit and do so consistently? So you must get your feet wet. You have to prove you can consistently fill customer orders. You must be able to project the future. What crops will you have and how much 4-6 months from now? And will they be the crops the customer wants? After you have made a crop decision (which only comes from market research suggested in later pages here), stick with one or two crops per season. At least for the first season or two. Gain a reputation for dependability.

You must get your price! You cannot stay in business without a profit. The only way you can get your price is to have the right crop available at the right time. If you are growing what everybody else is growing, your chances of making money are slim. The large hydroponic operations will take it away from you. Not to mention the average dirt-grower. This is very true with some foliage items such as ficus and croton. And it is particularly true with chrysanthemums which it seems everybody is trying to sell. Why not try for the market items which aren't on everybody's growing list? Why not research your market for those items which can give you that profit break? This is why this book recommends growing certain kinds of vegetables, especially the winter crops. Because you can go to your local market area and make deals on lettuce, cauliflower and Brussel sprouts and come out ahead of growers in California, Mexico and Florida. Your produce will be fresh - theirs will be too long from the field.

It isn't difficult to do this. Most produce and store managers will be happy to listen to your proposal. After all they're in the business to make money. All they'll want to know is are you dependable, can you do what you say you can do? Just keep in mind the market can be very huge. For example the Houston, Texas market is serviced not only by soil farmers but by a whole army of hydroponic growers. All of them are trying to satisfy this one market. Do they succeed in their efforts? Many times they don't. When we managed a nursery in Houston several years ago, there were occasions when even all these suppliers could not keep up with the market's demand. There were times we had to do without or else settle for something less in quality.

At the outset, two people can easily compete. They'll be able to handle their current operation of 1/3 acre or less. They'll be more conscientious. They'll put out quality plants and do it consistently. One of them can specialize in marketing - the other can handle the growing. As time goes by both of them will develop a reputation for quality and consistency. As their operation grows larger, they will find that their hydroponicum's output will increase at a relatively constant rate. This will enable them to accurately forecast larger and more profitable markets. By this time they will have others on their payroll.

Make a complete market survey before you start building. Check out all of the following: home-owned stores, supermarkets, national chains, retail florists, nurseries, farmer's markets, even flea markets and county fairs. We know of a man who does nothing else but sell at flea markets and county fairs. How about those little shops in outdoor malls, convenience stores, fast-food restaurants, high-class restaurants? The list is endless - everybody loves food and everybody loves plants. Check each one out. Find out what each usually runs short of and when. Ask them if they would rather have a more secure source of supply.

When approaching these people, be specific and make it short. Don't waste their time. Listen to their responses. If you're already growing and want to expand a little, take along some of your best samples. The prospective buyer will then have something more concrete to look at. listen to what these people have to say. Make notes on the interview later, after you leave. Don't try to remember - write it down. You may find the prospective buyer isn't interested in your fine African violets but would like to buy all the high-quality fern you can provide. Try to determine for yourself the retail prices on these items - they are on display for everyone to see. For example, if a large specimen fern is priced retail at $40, you will be able to wholesale it for $20 to $27. Quality fern sells for that and more.

If your goal is to grow quality vegetables, check out the restaurants, such as Chinese restaurants for bok choy. Remember? Check out the finer restaurants and ask the chefs if they'd like to have quality herbs. There are many ways to "open a market". After you've finished your survey and found the "soft" spots on the market, go to the buyers you have in mind and make the best deal you can. Once you've done all of this you'll be able to proceed with some confidence. And you can place your hydroponicum into full operation.

It doesn't all end there. This is just the beginning to a long and enjoyable career. And you still have a lot to learn because like in all businesses the markets always change. What's selling this season may not be so hot next year or even next season. But there are some predictables and you'll find them as you go along. If you keep your eyes open, you'll quickly see how your operation can mesh into a special niche of the market and hold its own in that niche. There are ways you can insure this.

MARKETING 1: You have to localize your operation.

Always remember you are competing with growers from all parts of the nation as well as countries outside our nation's borders. The only way you can beat them is to offer what they can't: freshness, nutrition, higher quality. And you must offer what the customer wants. Per capita consumption for processed vegetables is declining, and new diets are pointing customers to fresh vegetables. But the customer will only buy if he feels the food is fresh and nutritious. Yet less than five per cent of the buying public is aware of what constitutes a fresh and nutritious vegetable. In order to compete with the large grower, the small grower will have to look for markets which can't be serviced efficiently by the large grower and where price is not the only criteria. Such markets have been mentioned before - such as gourmet shops and restaurants, salad bars, delicatessens. Your own list of customers will come through local advertising, perhaps a roadside stand of your own. "Locally grown" advertising will be your biggest sales tool.

The average grower can prosper if he will locate near a large or medium-size city, have fast and dependable deliveries, maintain consistent production to fill the need, and learn to educate the public about nutrition and fresh vegetables. The same grower can do well if he offers plants and foliage and follows the above criteria. If you are not near a large city, you will need dependable, fast and low-cost transportation. (Large city = 100,000 +)

Here is where most growers fail: They usually have no problem producing a crop. But they have a poor or no marketing plan. Their production costs are too high. Their greenhouses are poorly designed. They often don't know the costs of production. Most of them don't even know what it costs them to set up their operation. They are in business but they don't know a thing about business. It should be obvious that in any business you would need to avoid such attitudes as these. So what's wrong with most people who go into hydroponics? They "love" plants! They don't realize that in order to succeed they must not only "love" plants but they must also sell them!

On what does price depend? Price depends upon the crop's appearance, its taste, and the price of your competitor's crop. If your competition scores high on these points, you will have a hard time getting your 20% above your competitor's price. When your competitor doesn't have a crop which has the above features, you can get your price and make a profit. But you must faithfully follow through on accepted marketing methods. When it comes to pricing your crop, use the following guidelines. Vegetables: the retail price will be 43-50% higher than your wholesale. Or about 30% less than retail will give you the wholesale price. For example if a plant normally retails for $9, it will usually wholesale for $6 (except for shrub and lawn crops). Suppose you are competing with field crops such as Mexican tomatoes. At the height of the season when the competitor's crop is at its prime you will price at about 10-15 cents higher per pound (for tomatoes). When your competitor's crop quality falls off, you can raise your price another 10-15 cents per pound. For foliage and potted plants the markup from wholesale to retail is around 100%. For example a wholesale cost of $4 will yield a retail price of $8 and more.

MARKETING 2: Selling Nutrition:

Most of all try to grow crops which are not in direct competition with field-grown crops. But if you must compete, do so by setting yourself apart from the others. Your product should offer the highest nutrition, be fresher, tastier. Establish your product as something very different, something quite distinctive and attractive. How do you do this? Find out what the customer is looking for. Normally the customer expects food which is fresher and crispier, locally grown and juicier, cleanly wrapped and packaged, picked while "vine-ripe". He doesn't want his tomatoes gassed to make them red. He doesn't want his cucumbers waxed to keep them "fresh". He wants produce whose shape is uniform and whose color is natural.

How do we educate the customer to nutrition? First direct your activities toward that percentage of the public which will pay for better nutrition. Start with better and more attractive packaging. Put your logo or label on every fruit or individual product. Identify yourself, stress the high nutrition and freshness of your product. The buyer wants to see your name and address on your logo and on the product. He feels you wouldn't sell such a product if it wasn't good. And you certainly wouldn't put your name on it. And if you package each fruit and vegetable, the buyer will think each is clean. Nobody has had a chance to finger them.

Some authorities say if we all ate greenhouse produce there wouldn't be a need for vitamin supplements. Most vegetables start losing their vitamin and food content within hours from the moment they are harvested. And cold storage doesn't stop the loss. Some vegetables will lose as much as 50% of their food and vitamin content the first day! **LET YOUR CUSTOMERS KNOW THIS. LET THEM SAMPLE YOUR PRODUCT.** Then you follow through. Have signs and posters at the point of sale which describe the benefits of your product, what it will do for the buyer. Large chain stores are now stressing nutrition and freshness. Consumers will rate those stores higher which feature such information. If you deal with stores whose managers are careless about the use of your signs, then rent space in a local paper in which you identify the stores which feature your produce. This works very well in small town weeklies. Don't forget to keep your logo active throughout your entire business - on your product, in your correspondence, in your advertising , on your truck.

You have to make it happen! You have to get the increased demand, the greater consumption, for your brand. Fortunately you can do this easily as well as cheaply. First provide in-store sampling. Contact USDA for information on the freshness of field-grown produce and draw up charts which compare their lack of nutrition to what your freshly harvested products offer. Don't name names; just list the general properties. Those tomatoes your competition has in the stores during winter are a good example. They might look fresh but that doesn't mean they are. Most likely they taste flat and have very little food value. Also be sure to concentrate on packaging and handling. Proper care with these two procedures will make for a more acceptable crop.

You can use point of sale posters which give instructions on how the buyer can get the most from his purchase. Perhaps you can include some recipes for the product's use. (Or you can give instructions on the care and feeding of a particular plant.) Since the buyer ranks nutrition right behind taste and freshness, he'll want this information. He depends upon you, the seller, for this information. He will pay for nutrition if he's sure of getting it. All of this can be done locally and at low cost. Some stores will be convinced to go along with you if you offer incentive plans such as: in-store demonstrations to customers, free samples to the buying public, initial money-back guarantees to store management to get your product started. You will take the risk if he will give it a chance.

Always keep this in mind: A lot of people are eating less meat and more vegetables. They are looking for their nutrition needs to be satisfied by you. Nutrition and freshness are not gained by increasing the product's ability to withstand longer shelf life but by getting the product to the customer as fast as possible. So you must schedule your crops in order to have constant "immediate" freshness. The ideal would be: as soon as the product ripens it's sold to a ready and eager buyer. As you can see the demand for the product is there. You just have to make the product available with high quality and on a consistent basis. Your production strategy will be based upon your marketing, because that's how you get your premium price which enables you to stay in business.

MARKETING 3: Marketing Analysis:

Don't be an amateur! You have to decide what business you are in. Then you have to determine what niche you wish to occupy. It won't do to say you're in the vegetable or plant business. You have to find out what markets exist or you can cause to exist. Then you have to specialize not only in particular plants but also in particular markets.

Failure to Plan = Total Failure! Here are some major points to consider before beginning in hydroponics: Have you analyzed your motives? Why do you want to go into hydroponics? If you don't like marketing you had better forget hydroponics as well as most other businesses. Have you done your research? Do you know what individual markets you are trying to reach?

No market is completely captured right away. Do you know how you're going to go about it? Have you written it down for future study? Have you researched to the point you know what individual crops you are going to grow? Do you know how to grow these crops?o. Are you (or do you have the ability to become) a good grower? When your operation becomes larger, your workers are not going to tell you what's wrong. You'll have to be consistent, watchful and aware.

Suppose you become successful? If you're selling something which is going very well, it won't take long before the competition finds out. What have you got up your sleeve when that happens? You will need to know what makes you successful and what you intend to do to stay successful.

Hydroponics will not fail you - if you do not fail hydroponics! To be successful means you are always thinking ahead - looking for new crops, new markets, new ideas. Your attitude is always that of the full-time professional. You're always fully prepared; you know the answers before you start.

How much of your budget should you allocate to marketing/advertising? At least 20%! And what types of advertising will you use? There are all kinds. One of the best is to offer free samples - wherever you find the customer. For example offer free slices of a hydroponic tomato.

Ask the prospective customer if it isn't the best tomato he's ever tasted. Then tell him how it's grown. Give away samples of foliage or a new flowering plant you're "thinking about" growing. Ask the customer what she or he thinks of it.

Decide exactly what type of market you wish to penetrate. Will it be wholesale or retail or both? Whatever the approach, let the individual you are calling on see you often and on a regular basis. Let him become accustomed to you, even perhaps looking forward to your visits. This will be especially true if you can help him with some of his problems. One of his problems is having desirable plants and vegetables delivered to him on a regular and profitable basis. Know the managers and owners of the wholesale/retail outlets you are contacting. Know them as human beings and treat them as such. You don't have to be "selling" them every time you see them. But you can be educating them to new products you have or ask them what they think of a new product you have in mind. **THIS IS LOW-COST MARKETING AT ITS BEST!**

Don't go overboard. Don't promise the moon. First determine minimum figures for production. Not what you hope for but what the minimum would be if you took adverse conditions into mind. If you can have reliable production and delivery based on these minimum figures, then as time goes by the figures will become more reliable. And your reputation will stand on promises made which you have kept. Again, premium prices only come after a product has been adequately promoted and advertised. After your name is well-known for the finest in quality, you'll have no trouble with competition undercutting your price. Just keep on stressing hydroponics's best features: locally grown, vine ripened, delivered fresh, right off the vine, picked ripe. There should be no restrictions on this type of product advertising, but check with state and local authorities anyway.

Formula for Success: Quality Plus Consistency Plus Promises Made and Kept. If you follow these dictates, things will only get better for you. Be creative; good things will happen. For example, like one supplier to a fast food franchiser in Maine who discovered that many of these places of business had never been approached by a grower. The grower in this case said that nine out of ten businesses he approached had never been asked before. Now this grower sells these same businesses his fresh produce at a higher price than they paid before. It makes sense. Most restaurants have to "clean" produce they have bought which has usually been shipped in form another state. They have a lot of waste. Our hydroponic grower sells produce which is fresh and has no waste. Therefor his price is fair and competitive.

Do you know your market? Do you know where it's located? Do you know what kind of people live in this market? If you know the answers to these questions, you'll begin to know what to grow. It may be that after analyzing a market close to you you'll decide on one which is further away. That choice may seem more attractive and profitable. But ask yourself: is this market a boom area or a stable one? Is it maturing or growing slowly? What about the market's economy? Have you gone around to the stores and seen what's on their shelves? Are there exotic items like European cucumbers, fresh herbs, unusual vegetables and fruits, unusual flowers and potted plants - all at reasonable prices? Or are these stores carrying the ordinary, the humdrum? How many expensive restaurants are located in the market area? Are there new shopping centers and other housing going up? Is the economic activity of the market area broad and stable or do the inhabitants rely on just one or two industries for a livelihood? What's the demand for and the quality of those crops now available in that market?

Remember: Hydroponic crops almost always sell for more than seasonal field crops. A very small percentage of the buying public buys for the quality you'll be able to offer. This will all change in time, but meanwhile you must find your special market for both premium and off-premium hydroponic crops. Are there seasonal changes in the market? There usually are. Find out about them.

What crops aren't available during certain times of the year? If you can grow them will they sell at a premium price? If there are preferred crops in this market area, find out when shortages occur and when the prices go up. You could arrange your growing schedule to capitalize on such events! **Never underestimate the competition!** Get bulletins from your agricultural agent. Find out about forecasts in other parts of the nation and the world. For example, imports for cut flowers are heavy right now. The market has become cut-throat. This is a good example of what imports can do to growers in a local market. So identify foreign and national growers for the crops you intend to grow. And adjust your activities accordingly. If your competitor (local or otherwise) has been in business for several years don't assume he doesn't know what he's doing. He wouldn't be in business if he was stupid! Find out what he's doing and how. But don't compete head-on with him. Find a different track. One more in keeping with your talents and more specialized in areas different than those of your competitor. **DON'T RUN HEAD-ON INTO BRICK WALLS!** Even competitors who have failed can be of help. Their mistakes can save you money. Often they've spotted trends in the buying public after it's too late for them to take advantage of them. Your agricultural agent can tell you who the good and bad growers are.

The buyer's time is valuable. So make appointments when you want to talk to them. Always get several opinions about each item on your survey. You'll get a better and more accurate consensus of opinions. Send everyone a thank-you note afterwards. You'll want to see them again after you start up your operation. When dealing with a buyer make certain you understand exactly what he wants, how he wants it and with what regularity. Bear in mind that you are a new face to him. He already has existing contacts on whom has grown to rely. Because of this you won't get a large percentage of his business right away. You'll have to patiently cultivate him. Of course you'll find ways to sell at retail. But when you wholesale it's entirely different ball game. It takes time to cultivate buyers or brokers. But it's worth it. **THE BUYER IS ALWAYS WATCHING YOU: CAN YOU DELIVER? IS IT WHAT HE WANTS? CAN YOU DO IT CONSISTENTLY?**

MARKETING 4: Marketing research is the most important thing you can do.

And for vegetables you implement it by using nutrition as your guideline. Before you can decide how you will approach a market, you must go into that market and get some questions

48

answered. Let's suppose you want to grow tomatoes. You will have to find out what the customer likes in tomatoes and what he's willing to pay. Perhaps the customer wants a tomato which is firm in texture, has very few seeds, is clean (wrapped), has excellent taste and has your logo on it. We said perhaps - you'll have to ask the customer to be sure. **DON'T ASSUME!** How are you going to get this information? By being in the store or at the market where the customer can be found. You could have a plate of your own freshly sliced tomatoes at hand. Offer the customer a taste and ask him some questions.

Here's where your ability to listen counts! Pay attention to what the customer says. You might ask the customer about the best recipe she ever used with hydroponic tomatoes. Write down everything she says - as fast as you can. She'll think her information is important (it is!) and give you some ideas which you can use later in your advertising approach. If a customer doesn't venture much information (and also if she does), put a puzzled look on your face as if you don't quite understand. The customer is then more likely to give you more information. Probably she will tell you the real opinions she has about tomatoes and about hydroponic tomatoes in particular. Ask the customer if she's noticed friends and neighbors buying hydroponic tomatoes. She may tell you how hydroponic tomatoes are used in her home. If the customer doesn't buy hydroponic tomatoes ask her how your product compares with what she normally buys. Then ask her what size tomato she prefers. Ask her if her husband ever buys tomatoes. Maybe she prefers doing that herself - and has her reasons for doing so. Try to find out those reasons.

Is the customer willing to pay extra for your quality? Ask her. Is she aware of the nutritional value of your tomato as opposed to the field-grown? If not, tell her. How does the customer buy tomatoes - by the pound or by the number? Would she buy more if she were assured they all were of the highest quality? Ask her why she's buying hydroponic tomatoes instead of the field-grown which are two shelves away. Does locally-grown mean anything to her? Is she annoyed with the way hydroponic tomatoes have been sold in the past? Does her family use more tomatoes in the summer than in the winter? If so, why? Is it because she's afraid winter tomatoes will be flat, won't have taste, won't be firm? Is she familiar with the non-hydroponic winter tomato? Does she know it's picked green, gassed to make it red, and shipped over a thousand miles to occupy the shelves at her market?

Define your target customer! Perhaps she's a mother who has purchased your tomatoes after sampling them. You've got to determine why she bought them from you. A target customer is one whom you've determined in advance to be the best likely prospect for your tomatoes. She doesn't have to have a lot of money. Many people who like a good tomato will buy tomatoes priced higher and which may be a bit beyond their budget's range. If you want to set up a marketing plan which will work, the opinions of the target customer are what you want. From the very beginning you should be interested only in the target customer. So you must set up criteria which accurately define that customer.

Once you learn how to listen, you'll be doing effective marketing research. You'll learn how to vary your questions; you'll learn not to ask questions which lead nowhere. You won't ask questions which require one-word answers. You'll ask questions which get the customer to talking. You'll let the customer search for a way out to describe how she feels. And if there's an emotional response, you'll follow it up to the end where you're likely to find some good ideas. Don't look for the "correct" answer. Don't look for agreement or flattery. Look for differences of opinion - ammunition which you can use later on. Be sure to interview all the target customers you can find. Remember to have your sampling large enough to have accuracy. Even with all your efforts you will learn the customer is never permanently yours. Your research will help. The customer has to be continually re-assured by your product that it will always be excellent and exactly what she wants.

The Big Six:

> 1. Determine what people want to buy.
> 2. What portion of that market can you acquire?
> 3. Is that portion large enough for you?
> 4. Who's the competition?
> 5. What price will the customer pay?
> 6. Can you produce the crop at that price for a profit?

MARKETING 5: Supermarkets sell 50% of the plants/flowers.

And some individual retailers are losing out! Because supermarkets are no longer the dumping ground for inferior plants. Large store chains are now paying more for quality and are ordering in advance. They're no longer shopping around after having made a contract. By the same token these large chains expect the grower to remain true to his contract. What's all this mean to you? You've already figured the large grower through his broker has got the supermarket business cornered? Wrong! Maybe it does take some extra effort to become a registered seller with the supermarket chain's home office. But the end results can be very gratifying to the small grower.

What are the problems involved in selling to supermarkets? For vegetables you only have to convince market buyers of your quality and availability. Other problems arise when it comes to foliage, flowers and plants. Supermarket managers want everything easily graded and packaged - like their shelves of canned goods and boxed cereal. Thus their stores can advertise by brand and size and set up competitive pricing. Flowers, foliage and plants are not so easily handled. Keep in mind the supermarket manager is looking for consistency in quality an uniform sizing. The biggest problem is deciding upon quality. What does the market manager mean by quality and what do you mean? Both of you will have to come to agreement in order to conduct profitable business relations.

Two other problems need to be resolved. Produce managers of a supermarket usually go on to bigger jobs within the company. This leaves a void in the produce department. Training programs are sometimes set up by the supermarket itself - but not always. Supermarket management and you need to get together on a consistent training program. Because there is a lot at stake here. The profits from a well-managed and fast-moving floral center in a supermarket can reach new highs when you consider that some stores gross as much as $400-$600 per square foot!

Displays are another problem. They are sometimes inconsistent with what you and the market manager intend them to be. A good display center must not only show off the product but also protect it from floor traffic. In order for supermarkets to better display your merchandise, the managers need to know about the profit potential. Your job is to help them see the light. Both of you will benefit in the long run.

Supermarket management looks to you to set the trends. You can't get off the hook by saying There's too much competition from overseas or too much foliage on the market. You will certainly find overproduction in some crops such as Dracaena (both massangeana and marginata) or Schefflera and Ficus benjamina. But why not take the hint. Learn to read the market and it's future. Check with other growers - see what they're doing. It's not necessary for you to do the same as they're doing. That kind of attitude is what bankrupts farmers! Look for the unusual, the coming trend or plant. Look for interesting plants which you can grow. Remember this: if a buyer can choose between a plant which is green only and another which is not only green but also has some flowers he, the buyer, is going to choose the flowering plant. He knows that most customers want indoor plants which will keep for a period of time. That customer wants clean foliage in clean pots. Most of all, he wants color! For example, try a new variety called Ficus nitida which is sold under the trade name of "GreenzGem". Try plants such as croton, anthurium, hibiscus. Hibiscus does quite well until it grows too large and has to be taken outside. Still the blooms from hibiscus flowering inside during the winter have few competitors. Try the unusual, the different. It's an excellent survival technique!

From all reports there is continual demand for foliage, flowers and plants. If you're not doing so well here, maybe you should look at your method of operation. Are you making a profit or just trading dollars? Trading dollars is no way to run a business. How about your marketing approach? Are you doing everything you can to let the world know what you're about? Have you been trying to find out what the customer wants (or thinks he wants) and then supplying it? One more thing, when dealing with supermarkets make sure they take your crops on time as agreed.

MARKETING 6: This is what successful marketing means:
1. Communication between you and the customer. What's said and what's unsaid.
2. Don't try to get back all your startup costs the first year. Be willing to amortize these costs over a period of years.
3. Don't let someone else decide what the customer wants or ought to want. Let the customer tell you what he wants.
4. Try to find out why competitors haven't put you out of business. Then figure out what they could do to put you out of business. **PLAN ACCORDINGLY!**

5. Innovate (putting new ideas to use) with care. Innovation will make you succeed and keep you ahead of competitors. But innovation without sober consideration can also break you.
6. Determine what share of the market is most profitable for you and price to make certain that market share comes to you.
7. Talk to your customers. Ask them what they like or dislike about the way you do business.
8. Assume your competitors know all about you and your plans and are conspiring what they should do. Then decide how you will react when and if a competitor decides to do something.
9. Look at your business from your competitor's point of view. Ask yourself what you would do to take business away from yourself. In defending yourself, ask yourself if you could have done better. What could you have done better?

DON'T ACCEPT SUCCESS AS THE FINAL WORD!

1. Do a market pre-test of all new ideas. Never give up looking for new ideas. It's the only way to survive!
2. Expansion - is it justified? Would you do better by more efficiently operating with what you have?
3. You are not a cost-plus business. The only customer who buys at cost-plus is the Pentagon.
4. Accept the fact that some ideas will work, some won't. Good business is comprised of both success and failure.
5. Adjust your prices to meet the competition - then keep them there. Don't be a price-cutter. It defeats your purpose.
6. Best credit setup: make your delivery, have the delivery receipt signed, and go to the front office to be paid.
7. Have your printer make up invoices which are consecutively numbered. Each invoice should be at least in duplicate if not triplicate. This prevents misunderstanding between you and your customer. It also looks a lot more business-like.
8. Don't display poor quality with good quality. The result depresses prices for both.
9. When setting up your marketing plan, don't make the quotas so large or the deadlines so close that you can't get to sleep at night worrying about them.
10. **KNOW ALL YOUR COSTS DOWN TO THE PENNY!**

How will you answer these questions from produce managers?

1. How much can I gross per square foot?
2. Will you give me consistent delivery and on-time?
3. What extra help are you going to give me.
4. Is your product going to be on hand all year round?
5. Why should I make extra space for your product?

6. Are you going to have other products which will bring in more customers?
7. Will you have price promotions on a regular basis?
8. What will you do about losses which I may experience with your product? (It is your responsibility to work with the retailer in curtailing such losses.)

MARKETING 7: Some ways to higher profits: a baker's dozen!
1. Keep an eye out for new cultivars by traveling to botanical gardens and other states and countries.
2. Watch for developments among growers in other regions of the country.
3. If you're selling retail in the growing area or the greenhouse, have a comfort and free coffee area for your customers.
4. Know where every item of your inventory is located - plants, tools, supplies, etc.
5. Keep a flow chart of where plants are growing and how they're moving through the growing area.
6. **MAKE BETTER USE OF SPACE.** Use double-tiered benches with fluorescent cool lamps under those benches to grow other crops such as African violets. The warmth from the lights will help the roots on the shelf above and raise greenhouse temperatures.
7. Keep a clean house with strict control of what's going on.
8. Some slow-release fertilizer placed in plants under HID lamps in the shipping room will be a great help in having plants market ready.
9. Propagate and produce under the best conditions possible by testing rooting medium on a regular schedule and keeping the temperature (for most plants) at 70 degrees F.
10. **Hire good help and pay them well.**
11. Hold open house for your customers every now and then. Invite the local news media to these events.
12. Have many outlets to insure selling a given crop.
13. Use a legal scale for vegetables. Make certain the customer gets his due.

What is Advertising?
1. It's a promise which the customer wants to be promised and in words he wants to hear. **BUILD YOUR MARKETING PLAN AROUND THIS IDEA!**
2. Your best ideas come from your customers - so listen to them. Advertising finds out what the customer wants but isn't getting.

Advertising finds out where the customer can be reached and how. Advertising analyzes future trends - what the customer might want in the future. When you know all of this, then advertise that you're the man who can fill these needs and desires. Just make certain you can and do. Even if you run out of product and have to buy it from someone else! Feature a plant of the month. Start a plant of the month club. Plant clumps of color outside your place of business.

If you can't furnish top quality and keeping characteristics in your plants, you'd be better off dumping them than trying to sell then at a lower price. The only time you can justify selling lower-grade products is when it's something like tomatoes which can be sold as "salad-grade" to institutions.

Because of the inability to find adequate labor and high automation costs to replace that labor, the medium-size grower is going out of fashion. We are now seeing a trend to either large or small growers. The latter are becoming more specialized. Small growers are beginning to place their marketing efforts toward retail outlets rather than wholesale. And small growers are no longer trying to compete with the large growers. Instead, in foliage and flowering plants, the small grower is seeking florist-type quality. In a word, the small grower is becoming more professional! Those growers who still make the old or traditional assumptions not only are holding back themselves but they are also holding back the industry. They reflect upon us all and the public does take notice.

MARKETING 8: An Interview with a Retail Florist:

MAYHILL PRESS: Where do you buy most of your plants?
FLORIST: I buy a lot from Holland and the Caribbean nations.
MAYHILL PRESS: Why is that? I mean why do you buy so much from abroad?
FLORIST: Because I have to. Local growers don't furnish what I need. And the quality and price of flowers and plants from abroad are hard to beat. The local growers say they can't compete at the prices I pay.
MAYHILL PRESS: Don't you buy anything from local growers? By local I mean growers within a fifty to one hundred mile radius.
FLORIST: Aside from poinsettias and a handful of others, I get all of my plants from distances far beyond what you mention.
MAYHILL PRESS: What about foliage?
FLORIST: Most of that comes to me from Florida and the Caribbean.
MAYHILL PRESS: What about freshness and quality?
FLORIST: I deal with a broker. If anything I order isn't up to my standards, I send it back and get full credit.
MAYHILL PRESS: What do you expect in freshness?
FLORIST: I expect all cut flowers to hold up for at least a week. Hopefully the same flowers will hold up for several days inside the customer's home.
MAYHILL PRESS: What would it take for you to switch your buying activities to the local grower?
FLORIST: I'd be happy to purchase all my plants and flowers from local growers if only to insure that my merchandise would be at the peak of freshness and quality.
MAYHILL PRESS: Do you think this would be profitable for the local grower?

FLORIST: I don't see why not. But to tell the truth I think most growers, at least in our area, aren't interested in learning how to compete with growers who ship in from long distances.

MAYHILL PRESS: What do you suggest they do?

FLORIST: They should learn to get out and hustle. They should make regular visits to all retail florists in their area. They should find out what the florists need and when they need it. Then they should grow for this market and maintain nothing but the highest quality. They should give service, service, service!

MAYHILL PRESS: Give us an example.

FLORIST: Take cut flowers. Holland growers sell them by the ton. Not only abroad to us but to their own customers at home. Growers in Holland are willing to work on a lower margin of profit in order to get the market to come to them.

MAYHILL PRESS: You're aware that Europeans buy a lot more flowers, especially the cut variety, than Americans?

FLORIST: I'm very much aware of that fact. But Americans can be educated to live with more flowers.

MAYHILL PRESS: What about foliage? Why can't the local grower furnish that?

FLORIST: I don't see why not. But rarely do I see a local grower coming by to ask me to buy his foliage.

MAYHILL PRESS: What would you really like to see the local grower do?

FLORIST: What I'd like to see is a local grower who can grow specifically for me. Who will keep in touch on a regular needed basis and always make sure he can deliver. A grower who offers quality and service. From what I understand, success goes to those who offer just a little bit more. Again, I've seen very few local growers who are willing to make such commitments.

MAYHILL PRESS: It all boils down to dependability and quality?

FLORIST: Doesn't everything? Wouldn't you rather deal with someone who had these characteristics?

MAYHILL PRESS: Do you really think that if a grower came to you and offered to grow what you need, when you need it and make it of the highest quality, that you would switch over and do business with him?

FLORIST: You bet! What's more important, if this grower can offer his product at near competitive rates, he'll soon see his sales go up. And that's not only includes me but all the other retailers in the area.

MAYHILL PRESS: What about supermarkets?

FLORIST: Please! Still the more they sell, the more I sell. It's contagious.

MAYHILL PRESS: So the local grower can fit into that picture.

FLORIST: Supermarkets are just as happy as anyone else to get quality and service.

Here are further tips in dealing with the retail market:

1. Must have flexibility. Be able to supply lesser or greater amounts when necessary. Have the ability and facility to produce such amounts.
2. Have ample qualified help. Be certain you have the necessary experience to grow specific plants. Be able to provide on-site help with displays and signs which give plant information at the time of sale. Have an educational program set up not only for your own employees but also for the retailer's employees.
3. Be consistent on pricing and claims policy for damaged/returned goods

MARKETING 9: You and the Buyer:

Growers who are more concerned about costs than they are of quality will soon find themselves by-passed by the more knowledgeable buyer. Most buyers know US growers haven't had to compete in such highly competitive markets as those which exist in Europe. American growers aren't aggressive enough when it comes to getting more attention in wholesale and retail markets. They'll soon find themselves on the short end of the stick when it comes to satisfying customers' needs and desires.

Some domestic growers are saying that foreign growers ruin the domestic market. This argument won't hold water. It's just a smoke screen to cover the grower's lack of attention to good marketing procedures. It's an excuse for pure laziness. What little marketing these growers do pursue is either poorly conceived or ineffectively done. The plain truth is there are too many market areas - especially for floral products - which aren't touched at all! And it's not just the grower who's to blame. Supermarket and retail managers can shoulder the major portion of that blame. Too often these people don't realize the profit they're losing when they allow flowers to get too old before they throw them out. A produce manager wouldn't do that. Also a lot of retail outlets don't have enough flowers on display. They don't have the flowers grouped in significant eye-catching displays. **LARGE COLORFUL DISPLAYS SELL FLOWERS - NOT ADVERTISING.** That said, it's time to recognize that some supermarket managers are well aware of what makes flowers move in quantity from the grower to the final buyer. What used to be an impulse item has now become the center of attention in some supermarkets whose managers have the savvy and aggressiveness to push their products.

More importantly their suppliers (growers) are also in on the act. Such up-and-coming growers not only help train the store personnel but also make sure there's a descriptive tag on every plant. As one of the largest growers has said, he wouldn't think of shipping a plant or a pot of flowers unless it had a tag which included complete self-care inscribed thereon! He says if you want a customer to like exotic flowers and plants you have to first educate him on its proper care. The bonus comes when this same customer returns to buy more of what might be new and different.

The name of the game is repeat sales! You get these from knowledgeable customers, not dunces. Who educates the customer? You do! And so does retail management. You're both in this together. For example, some supermarkets include pictures of the flowers and plants they're featuring when they run a newspaper ad. A few are including instructions for feeding and care of the featured plants. In this way the supermarket is becoming the source of information for the prospective customer. A few markets are hiring people who know something about plants and who know how to sell them. But problems still persist. Too often flowers and plants are kept at the wrong temperatures for them to hold up over a long period of time in the store. They're transported in trucks whose temperatures are too low. Also some market managers still try to order at the last minute and expect the grower to magically come up with what they need. Other managers are beginning to plan their floral and plant promotions months in advance. This enables the grower to offer better quality at a lower price because he can plan and schedule ahead.

It's clear that supermarket managers are catching on fast. They're determined to succeed. And you, the grower, in order to succeed, must work with that manager. You must supply him with the necessary materials. This not only includes what to grow for him but helping out with advertising programs and in the store at point-of-sale displays. And you must convince the marketer of the value of large colorful displays. There's plenty of room for expansion for marketing a plant or floral product. **The key words are: educate and promote.**

Once the customer understands plants and their care, he'll buy more of them. The reason flowers and plants are so popular in Europe is because the ultimate buyers have been educated to want more of these products in their offices and homes. To the European, plants and flowers are as necessary as food.

MARKETING 10: Giving Added Value to Every Sale:

The old adage that you have to spend money to make money is truer now than it's ever been. If you don't advertise your wares how do you expect to attract the attention of prospective buyers? Too many growers have too long gone it alone in this phase of marketing. What's needed is more and more growers to band together and pool their advertising dollars for the common effort. But that's not likely to happen from where we sit. Growers have yet to get the message of cooperative marketing. In contrast the beef industry advertises continuously. Pork producers sell their product with loud acclaim. Raisin and almond growers are having a field day. By constant repetition alone these producers manage to drum up business on a large scale.

This is what our industry needs. But what can you, the individual grower, do about it? That is while you're waiting for other growers to get the idea. First you have to have an approach to growing which is systematic. Second your business philosophy must be one which emphasizes quality as well as service. Third you must have tight control on your production methods and this includes keeping greenhouses and surrounding areas clean. One way to control production is to grow fewer cultivars (plants) and more volume with the ones you do choose to grow. This will entail having your buyer contracts set up for the entire year. Then you'll have to position yourself to reach certain harvest dates. From seed to sale - you must keep everything under control in order to be successful.

You must furnish perks for your customers. For example if you're selling small plants such as 3-4 inch material it would be a good idea to furnish your retail seller with material on capillary-matt fitted trays. This type of tray will make it easier for the seller's people to water the plants and keep them fresh. The tray could be returned to you when the plants have been sold. Why not add more value to each sale? You could pack the plant better or set it in a more attractive pot. You could furnish higher quality plants (we hope you're already doing that). Anything which makes the customer think he's getting more for his money. For example you could use a hinged three or four pot display which would be easier to carry and which might prompt the customer to buy the entire kit. Instead of selling one plant you could sell three or four at time! One grower came up with this idea: he furnishes a "garden" of six or more different plants which are placed together in one carrying basket. His success with this one idea was phenomenal! Herbs would be good for this.

Watch what your customers are buying. Find out what they do with the containers when they get home. You may find some surprises. When I was a manager of a large nursery in Houston, we constantly trained our floor personnel to always suggest an attractive pot to go along with each and every plant purchase. Not only did this increase our profit but it also bound our customers more closely to us. Try it. Your customers will appreciate your suggestions. Also try some innovating of your own. If you can add value to a sale without substantially increasing your costs you've made a thankful customer who will come back to you again and again. Added value also includes helping your retail customer keep track of sales. Have him dump material which is old or poor-looking. Then reimburse him for the loss. But make certain his employees are trained to take care of the plants - even if you have to do the training. You could lose a lot if the employees don't know what they're doing.

MARKETING 11: Who is the Customer and What does he Buy?

Advertising works primarily with this premise: tell the customer you're going to tell him, tell the customer, tell him you've told him - over and over again. Repetition, done wisely, is the essence of good advertising. It's also the essence of conditioning. If many Americans don't think of buying plants and flowers as their European counterparts do, then what does it take to induce them to change their ways? Repetition. Repetition. Repetition! Over and over again. We all need to be reminded often to get us to do certain things. We have to do it to ourselves in order to be sure we don't forget something we want to do.

Tell the public what makes flowers and plants so necessary - why they should be a daily part of our lives. Make the idea something special, something a person should always keep in mind. Use visual displays - use verbal advertising. Attract the viewer's attention. Some customers buy flowers and plants out of tradition - they've always done it, especially for holidays. How many of you invariably buy a poinsettia for Christmas even when you're telling yourself it isn't necessary? What we want to do is to turn this singularity into a habit practiced throughout the entire year. Other customers will buy on occasions other than holidays or family events. Or on the spur of the moment while passing through a shopping center. Here is where you can find a lot of business if you slant your marketing endeavors in the customer's direction. There's also a large group of people who seldom buy plants or flowers. This group may be difficult to convince, but this is where a huge market area exists. It's up to you to find a way to get this potential customer to buy from you.

Perhaps new customers can be captured by offering different but interesting plant varieties. Varieties which haven't been seen before. Stress in all your advertising that plants and flowers are for decorating. That they should be a part of everyone's home. Not just for Christmas or Easter or Mother's Day - but for everyday. As a part of one's lifestyle!

Always bear in mind who your real competition is. It's not from other countries. It's not even from other states. It's for the spendable dollar which every consumer controls. Your competition is everything else which is being advertised in newspapers, magazines or television. Your job is to make flowers and plants more interesting than any other product. There are nearly 80 million affluent individuals who can be targeted. Those citizens who were born in the late forties and through the early sixties are prime prospects because they fall into distinct groups. You can put money in your pocket if you know the difference between nesters, materialists and self-stylers. Since the nesters are struggling to get along, you should target the other two groups for sales.

What kind of argument will appeal to the self-stylers? Aesthetics and quality is what they desire. These people want those things which will make their lives more interesting and fulfilling. They won't be attracted to the old sentimental images we've used in the past. They will be attracted to new types of plants. They will enjoy the exotic, which doesn't necessarily mean orchids. It does mean some of the new cultivars which are interesting and sometimes spectacular. Where do the self-stylers shop? Boutiques, specialty shops, anything which might be taken as upscale.

What about the materialistic crowd? They're the easiest to sell. Simply inform them that buying flowers and plants is the right thing to do. Everyone should have them in his home. Since materialists like to be with the in-crowd, they'll most certainly want to do the right thing. All you have to do is to keep telling them that which keeps them in the in-crowd. The problem is nobody is telling them. Our industry has, until recently, forgotten to ask the customer to buy. Before you purchased this book, we had to tell you over and over again that it was the right thing to do. That it was important that you know more about hydroponics. That your future would have to rest on a solid bed of knowledge. There's nothing unusual about this procedure. This is how anything, new or old, is sold. We all have to be reminded.

MARKETING 12: Handling, storing, shipping:

Storage of hydroponic vegetables defeats the purpose of growing vegetables hydroponically. Smart management will try to have the market ready when the crop is ready. But sometimes storage for a brief time is necessary. To do this temperature and humidity must be correctly maintained. Storage of tomatoes should be at temperatures above 55 degrees Fahrenheit (F), a little higher for additional ripening, a little lower for fruits fully ripened. Temperatures above 32 degree F will cause some loss of redness. The humidity storage range should be 80-90%. Too much light will cause already ripened fruit to become soft. If you want good shelf life at the market, ripe tomatoes should not be stored for more than four days. Generally the storage temperature for ripe tomatoes can be between 32 to 38 degrees F.

Lettuce at harvest should be taken immediately into a cool area where the lettuce can be trimmed and packaged. Lettuce is notorious for not having a long shelf life. According to some authorities, the best method is to wrap each head in an open-top polyethylene bag. This will enable you and the market manager to sprinkle water on the head when needed. The European cucumber must be shrink-wrapped and stored at a temperature of 55 degrees F, a humidity of 95%. Cucumbers should not be stored with other vegetables which produce ethylene. Fruits like tomatoes and melons will cause cucumbers to turn yellow. Nor should cucumbers be shipped with such vegetables. The best methods for pre-cooling the above vegetables are considered to be vacuum cooling for lettuce, and air which has been refrigerated for tomatoes and cucumbers.

When you ship your crop you must inform the carrier the conditions under which the crop must be maintained. This includes proper temperature as well as handling. Cucumbers will last nearly two weeks at 50-55 degrees F and a humidity of 95%. Ripe tomatoes will last only 3-5 days at 35-45 degrees F and a humidity of 90%. Leaf lettuce has a storage life of 4-6 days at 32 degrees F and a humidity of 95%. Head lettuce will last a week or so longer. The carrier must know these facts and be able to furnish the appropriate equipment.

Packaging is all-important. Like advertising it helps sell your crop. Since packaging technology attempts to provide boxes and containers which will fit on the internationally recognized pallet size of 47 1/2 inches by 39 1/3 inches, the standard vegetable container will be about 15 3/4 inches by 11 4/5 inches or 19 3/5 inches by 15 3/4 inches. These translate into 40 cm by 30 cm and 50 cm by 40 cm. As noted before, you should package all your plants and/or vegetables. On the package should be information which tells the customer what he needs to know - and things you want him or her to know. Vegetables should stress the cleanliness of hydroponic culture, the great flavor and nutrition - above all, their freshness. Get yourself a logo. What's that? It's sort of a trade mark - a special design for your product and no one else's. Copyright it. Package all vegetables in polythene bags to keep them clean from contamination and customer handling.

What about plants? This is a very large market. But not many growers package for this. Be different. Remember what we said about daffodils? Narcissus, tulips, hyacinth? Yes, we know packaging is pretty common for these. But why not come up with a new twist, find a way to put your stamp on everything you sell? This business takes creative imagination just as much as any other business. Look around at everyone else. See what they're doing and try to come up with something that will attract more customers.

Harvesting carts should be designed to facilitate the harvest. Workers must be trained to take proper care of the fruit or the plants. The ideal is to minimize damage at all steps in the harvesting program. Also, since your identifying logo is on each fruit or plant, it should also be on the outside of the box being used for shipping. Don't rely on the wrapping or packaging of the vegetable to keep it from being contaminated by outside gas or the types of fruits which produce such gas. If you have to ship long distances, it's sometimes best to subject your plants to a short period of stress before being shipped. This will help insure their survival.

What you must do when plants drop their leaves during shipping: Or any other time? Plants will drop their leaves when drastic changes occur. Ethylene is a culprit during the shipping process because often growers make the mistake of shipping plants with others which give off ethylene. Ethylene is a pollutant in the air around us.

Motor exhaust alone will cause plants to drop their leaves. Somewhat higher than normal concentrations of ethylene are found in supermarket warehouses where ethylene is used to ripen fruits such as tomatoes and melons. Another thing which will cause plants to drop their leaves is water stress (sometimes called shattering). So will low light and temperatures which are too high. Plants, like humans, cannot stand much stress. How do you reduce ethylene exposure? Use electric fork lifts in the docking and warehouse area. To avoid stress over long shipping distances, keep the temperature at 50 degrees F. You can also apply silver thiosulfate before shipping. Use a foliar spray of 1/2 - 1 ounce of concentrate per gallon of water. Let the spray run off the leaves and do this about two weeks before you ship. At the same time use some brand of spreader-sticker to help keep the silver thiosulfate on the leaves.

CHAPTER 6

THE BAG TECHNIQUE: Most used System in the U.S.

For those who want to start out fast. This is the easiest and least complicated way of growing hydroponically. The bags can be either vertical or the lay-flat type. The vertical bags hold 1/2 - 3/4 cubic foot of material; the lay-flat hold about 2 cubic feet. The vertical bags usually contain a mixture of peat moss and vermiculite whereas the lay-flat bags usually are filled with agricultural rockwool. The vertical bags are normally used for one plant such as a tomato plant. The lay-flats hold two or more plants. Most bags are made from 4-mil black polythene plastic. The bags are placed upon a thin sheet of polythene plastic (white in summer, black in winter) - this prevents the roots from growing outside the bag. Some growers are now using the double-bag system: black bag inside a white bag. Why? Because the white outer bag reflects the sunlight and helps keep the root system cool in the summer. Two-bag setups are also used to prevent algae from growing on the inside of the bags. Tests indicate that plants grow faster and are healthier in the two-bag system. Still, many growers use the black bag only.

Media used in containers of this sort range from 1/2 peat moss and 1/2 vermiculite, to peat-lite (commercial name), and a bark with wood chips (avoid cedar, eucalyptus, walnut and redwood). Bark media should have about 20% sawdust, shavings or bagasse in order to have enough water retention capacity. Most wood chips are acidic; if at all possible they should be composted before using. Bark's advantage over other media is that it can last through several crops. Others, like vermiculite, collapse after some use. Sawdust needs extra nitrogen to keep it from robbing the plants of food.

The requirements for a good growing medium in this kind of hydroponics are: must be lightweight, give good root aeration, have good water and nutrient holding capacities, be free of toxic elements and soil-born diseases. Price and geography will determine what you use. Vermiculite and sawdust must not be used by themselves as they hold too much water. Rice hulls do not have enough water-holding ability - they should be mixed with something else which does hold water. The advantages of the bag method are: nutrient solution is never out of balance because it is never recirculated, media like bark can be used over and over again (large growers don't recommend this), bag containers are easier to install, lightweight and easy to handle and can be used inside or outside where needed. Most importantly the medium in the container holds the nutrient and water satisfactorily and diseases are not a problem because the bags are not connected with one another. **A BAG SYSTEM IS AN OPEN SYSTEM.**

How are the plants fed and watered? In the beginning, by hand. Later when economically feasible, by polythene tubing (usually black) which goes from one bag to the next. Some growers used ring drip systems (a ring in every bag) or spray sticks. For up-right bags, the 90 degree spray sticks or the ring drippers are used. The ring setup is expensive. For lay-flat bags, single tubes of polyethylene which look like spaghetti are used for a wetting pattern at the point of contact. This is good for finely-textured media which will conduct the nutrient fluid laterally. The nutrient solution must be distributed in an even manner. The entire medium must be uniformly wet throughout. Of course your choice of which system to use will depend upon the crop and medium used. The prime factors for media are: porosity, texture, and area to be wetted.

The container and the medium: Both have to be specific.

Making a profit can be greatly enhanced if you know how to choose the correct container and with the correct medium mix. We all know that he who holds the watering hose holds our profits. What a lot of us fail to understand is that if the container and the enclosed medium do not match a plant's growing characteristics, our profits also go down the drain! Water and medium go hand-in-hand. Yet very few growers and their employees understand the nature of watering and how to do it correctly. Since the roots of the plants get their water and air from the medium area immediately surrounding them, it's very important that we understand containers, the medium which goes into those containers, and how we growers should handle them both.

Each plant has its own media needs. You or your supplier should fit the mix to the plant. A good growing mix should have 65-90% porosity and the available water should be from 20 to 40%. Therefore, unless you prepare your own mixes, you should purchase commercially prepared mixes from a supplier whose reputation you know is secure. Do not buy according to price - always get the best you can. Peat moss, as we have seen, may become a dwindling resource. You will have to find other substitutes such as perlite or agricultural rockwool or go altogether to NFT. Though authorities disagree, some saying commercial mixes are best and others saying you should prepare your own, one thing is certain. **YOUR SURVIVAL DEPENDS UPON HOW YOU HANDLE THE MEDIUM!**

The answer also lies in how you place the medium in the container. A large container can have its medium more tightly compressed. But anything less than a 6-inch pot will require lighter packing in order to keep the hydroscopic and total porosity variables in line. Smaller grained mixes can be used in larger pots, but don't use them in 4-inch or smaller pots! Instead use larger grained material and soak it in water before filling the pot. **REMEMBER: THE SMALLER THE POT THE LOOSER YOU PACK AND THE LIGHTER THE MIX.**

As an afterthought: Only that water which is held between medium particles can be made available to the plant. A plant can't pull away water which is chemically bound too tightly to the medium particles. This so called hydroscopic water is quite high in organic mixes such as peat. It's very possible that at least one-third of this hydroscopic water is not available in peat mixes even after drainage! **Moral:** Watch water content in such mixes.

Rockwool has undergone increasing scrutiny as a replacement for what seems to be dwindling peat supplies from Canada and other regions. A well-known successful grower thinks rockwool is better than NFT - when nutrient management is considered. The Dutch love to use rockwool. But not all is wine and roses. Rockwool, though sterile when manufactured, can be a haven for insect and pathogen pests. Also an artificial water table can develop within the rockwool. Why are a lot of growers turning to rockwool as a medium? Because of the ease of growing and the control you can have over the medium. Rockwool soaks up a lot of water. This eliminates worry about moisture and nutrient at the root zone. Still the grower must be aware as to how long the moisture will last. The plants won't tell him until it's too late. Care, as with anything else this side of paradise, is the criteria to go by.

Another medium which is drawing special attention is Oasis foam. This medium requires close attention because of the way in which it drops in pH. Also more and more media companies are offering pre-filled flats, pots, hanging baskets and other containers at slightly higher prices than what they charge for their media mixes. Thus the small grower can save time and labor by ordering these containers already filled with his designated mix or medium. You save on the labor of filling your own containers and you save by not having to order the media and the containers separately.

Some foliage potting mixes:

For plants requiring high water-holding capacity:
2 parts sphagnum peat moss
1 part horticultural vermiculite
1 part horticultural perlite

For plants requiring good drainage and less water retention:
1 part sphagnum peat moss
1 part horticultural perlite
1 part Douglas fir bark

Getting started: So now you can see how you can start out on a "shoestring" as compared to what you might have to invest otherwise. Like all businesses, this section suggests you start out as cheaply as possible, perhaps using the sand/gravel technique. Or if you wish, the bag technique. All of this can be done by starting out in early spring and reaping as much profit as possible by fall when you can then invest in building a greenhouse which is thoroughly discussed in Section Two. As in all businesses, you have to invest something in order to get started. At least now you have some basics for starting out in this business. And Section Two will give you more information on just about anything you would ever care to know about hydroponics.

Growers are innovative people - they have to be. Perhaps you'll have to start out by just scooping out a trench in the ground - as discussed earlier. Or maybe you'll be able to start with the bag technique. In any case, the goal is the same for all of us: beautiful and bountiful crops which sell easily. Though we propose potted plants and foliage for starting out, this is not to say you can't do quite well with vegetables. It just takes a little longer. Many growers do very well with tomatoes and lettuce, especially when they have a year-round operation. That's why you want to erect a greenhouse as soon as possible.

According to one authority, newcomers to hydroponics can make money with bedding plants, perennials, hanging baskets and pre-finished plants. Poor choices for the newcomer would be: poinsettias, roses, pot mums and foliage. But to each his own. Your success will often depend upon your location. But even if your location is not the best, just keep in mind you can ship a pound of tomatoes, etc., anywhere in the United States for very low rates. And off season prices can easily offset transportation costs. In any case even when you get your greenhouse up and fully complete you will still grow what your markets dictate.

Bits of information which you can use:
Other media to use: agricultural rockwool, marble chips, pebbles, rice hulls, sand, granite chips, pumice, haydite, cinders (check for pH and toxicity).

Drip system of watering? Yes when you can afford it.

For sand/gravel systems: they dry out faster than soil does. Watering is usually done two or more times a day, depending upon the weather. Spread your dry nutrient on the surface and water in only enough water to keep the medium moist. Sterilize the medium between plantings - try to avoid the use of formaldehyde. Your nearest supplier can help you with this.

Plants get 40% of their nourishment from the air around them (carbon dioxide). So air circulation is important. Blooming time will be dictated by the amount of light available.

If sand/gravel beds dry out too fast, you usually have too much sand in the medium. Cover with a layer of pea gravel. This will also help to check the growth of algae.

When you remove plants from sand/gravel beds, be sure to take out all the roots. Don't leave any organic material behind and don't disturb the medium too much.

Are you growing annual flowers in beds for cut-flower production? Start in vermiculite seed trays and then transplant to the beds.

In hot weather place lettuce seeds in a refrigerator for 24 hours before sowing. Do not place in the freezing compartment.

Peat moss must be allowed to soak for 24 hours, then squeezed of excess moisture. Use warm water for this. Store afterwards in a tightly closed bag for future use.

Polythene plastic comes in various sizes and thicknesses. The most common for greenhouse cover is mil 12 which is 100 feet long and 40 feet wide. In some cases you will be able to use a thinner sheet: an example of this would be the inside thermal layer which hangs beneath the outside layer or cover.

SECTION TWO

COMMERCIAL HYDROPONICS AND BEYOND

CHAPTER 7

THE GREENHOUSE

Where the Real Money Is.

In Section One of this manual we discussed the features of the modified Bengal System of hydroponics. This entails the use of sand/gravel beds which, when properly operated, can produce hydroponic crops in abundance. The Bengal System is the simplest and most inexpensive way of getting started. But as we suggested most growers in the United States now prefer the bag technique which is used for both pots and bags. To further your profits to the limit, a greenhouse is needed, whether you use sand/gravel, bag or any other technique. This chapter will be devoted entirely to the greenhouse. At first we shall deal with a low-cost design, including drawings, detail and building costs. Next we shall discuss the exact costs of stocking the greenhouse - or growing area - with enough plants to do the job. We shall use the bag or pot method for this. For those who really want to learn as much as possible about hydroponics and who may want to go commercial, Section Two will include details on all aspects of hydroponic growing.

To get the high out-of-season prices, you need a greenhouse. At the end of this chapter you will find diagrams of a greenhouse which has been designed to withstand high winds. Here are the rules which were followed in designing this type of greenhouse:

1. The structure must be self-sustaining in all climates and weather.
2. One must be able to water and feed without power, if necessary.
    a. For those who have the necessary terrain altitude drop (at least 40 feet), a ram jet will be a welcome addition.
    b. All water lines will be under ground - below the freeze line.
3. Must be able to heat the structure without power, at least to a minimal degree. This will entail:
    a. Beds on the ground.
    b. Black plastic under beds and under sand and gravel walkways.
    c. In some cases, solar drums (55 gallon drums filled with water and painted black n the outside) will be placed along the northern side of the greenhouse. See 3 ft (or smallest) bed in diagram - place drums in this area.
    d. Where tables are used, solar "casks" should be placed below.
4. Must be able to cool the structure without power - in most cases by raising the sides to allow breezes to flow through.
5. Must be able to withstand hail. Monsanta 603 mil 6 is strong and in many cases will do the job - but it will not withstand hail. There are three ways to go here. One, use Monsanto 603 mil 6 and hope for the best. Two, use a chicken wire plastic "sandwich". This is done with 1 or 2 inch wire mesh sandwiched between two sheets of plastic and is placed on the top for the roof. And three, buy very strong

hail-resistant plastic from Northern Greenhouse Sales, Box 42, Neche, ND 58265 or Box 1450, Altona, Manitoba, R0G-0B0, Canada.

6. The structure must be able to withstand wind.
   a. Penta treated 1x4x16 battens along the base to hold down plastic sides.
   b. Supporting posts all treated and sunk four feet in the ground. **WE WANT THIS STRUCTURE TO LAST AT LEAST TEN YEARS!**

7. Also consider the following when installing the power-heat package: the houses must be connectable, thereby affording a continuous series of houses which can be readily climatized.

8. Must be a workable house but at the same time fully occupied with growing plants.

9. Must be low enough in cost in order to have funds for the first house at the end of the first growing season.

The following data refers to the drawings at the end of this chapter:

FIGURE 1: This is a general overview of the greenhouse. It is 30 ft wide, 96 ft long. The sides are 6 ft high and the center ridge is 8 ft high (except for snow areas in which case the center ridge might be 10 or 12 ft high).

A door may be placed at each end - in our drawings we recommend one door at one end. This is an optional feature. At the end of the first growing year, after the first house has been erected, enough profits should have been generated to enable the grower to purchase the heating/cooling package (discussed in cost specifications later) so that the grower can go into the second winter with a house ready to grow all winter long. In addition to this enough profits should also have been generated to allow the grower to attach a second growing house (not heated/cooled) for the coming season. Of course the sooner you can put up a house the sooner you can generate more profit. In other words, the house can be erected before any profits have been earned. **HOWEVER THE PRIMARY PURPOSE OF THIS BOOK IS TO HAVE YOU START FROM SCRATCH AND PAY AS YOU GO.**

FIGURE 2: This is the side view of the greenhouse. Note that all posts are sunk four feet into the ground. This is to help the structure withstand high winds. Except for the four end posts which are originally ten ft long with five inch tips, all side posts are also ten ft long but with four inch tips. All center ridge posts are twelve ft long with five inch tips. (Five inch tip means a round pole with a five inch diameter at the smallest end.) **ALL POSTS ARE WATER-PROOFED AND PLANTED FOUR FEET DEEP.**

This greenhouse calls for a double layer of plastic on all surfaces -top, sides and ends. All wood is therefor enclosed in dry air. If you have the extra cash then buy treated lumber for ridge, eave and end plates - but this design will suffice without extras. All water condensed on the inner layers of plastic will run down to the ground. Therefore no wood should get wet.

In addition, as a precaution, you can use an inflation blower. This is an ordinary economical squirrel cage setup which will blow air continuously between the sheets of plastic (which are 3-4 inches apart) and keep them dry and separated. This will also help to keep the top sheets from rubbing too much against their supporting wires. One more thing: to ensure good air circulation inside the greenhouse, construct a plastic tube, 1 1/2 feet in diameter and run it under and along the top center ridge from one end of the greenhouse to the other. Make certain it is attached to the blower air supply. Also make air holes all along the bottom side so the air will blow out into the entire greenhouse.

The bottom batten (referred to on drawing by **) is tied down with bolts. When you want to raise these battens (each 16 ft long), you simply unbolt them, turn them inward and hook to the hook on the top inside. This will let any moisture or rain coming from the roof to drop off harmlessly without getting caught inside the raised batten and plastic. The same can be done with the inside batten and plastic. Just raise it to the top and hook accordingly.

Each bottom batten (both inside and outside) is anchored to the other with a long bolt and nut (the bolts run through the posts) - during bad weather or for winter usage. At the end of each batten (outside on the outside batten and facing inside on the inside batten) there is an eye hook. Simply unbolt the battens, then raise inward to the other hook at the inside top batten and then hook to hold.

When attaching plastic to these battens, use a staple gun or, better still, use 1" lath to tie down to the batten. Figure 2 shows the battens as A -- but remember the drawing just shows the outside. There is a duplicate set on the inside. And the bottom batten is the only one you raise. The top batten is permanent -- it anchors both the roof plastic (which should be drawn tight before tying down) and also the side wall plastic. Note that the top battens are anchored an inch or so below the eave ridge boards to allow for moisture drippage and air passage.

Please note that only Monsanta 603 Mil 6 is used for the top layer and the west or south side (if greenhouse runs north and south, then the side in question is the west side; if it runs east-west, the side in question is the south side. Most operators run their greenhouses east-west.) Also Monsanta 603 Mil 4 is used for the inner roof layer and the inner side layer. The Visaqueen Clear Mil 6 (see greenhouse cost specifics) is used for both layers on the east or north side and for both ends.

One more thing in Figure 2: The eave ridge - 2x4x16 - runs perpendicular to the ground and for the full 96 feet.

FIGURE 3: This shows permanent batten tie downs both top and bottom. The top batten also holds the top roof plastic tightly in place. The tighter you draw the plastic on the outer layers, the longer the layers will last. When the time comes to instal the heating/cooling package, some easy modifications can be made at each end to facilitate the placement of the equipment.

FIGURE 4: Please note the placement of all poles. The center ridge poles stand eight feet above ground, the side posts and end posts stand six feet above ground and the intermediate end poles (placed at fifteen feet from the side stand approximately seven feet above ground.

VERY IMPORTANT: In order for this house to hold roof supporting wires tight, you must place all ridge boards perpendicular to the ground - on their edges, so to speak. The top 2x4x16 timbers at the ends of the house must be laid flat (wide side down) in order to get the strength to hold back on the tension created by the wires. We are referring to "P" in the drawing. The "Q" timbers are laid perpendicular to the ground because the lower layer of roof plastic doesn't have to be as tight as the top layer. See Figure 9.

FIGURE 5: This figure shows the pole placement - all on 16 foot centers - and the wire placement - all on 2 1/2 foot centers. Note again "B", the end posts. These are 5 inch tips whereas the side posts, though of the same length, are 4 inch tips. Note also that all ridge timbers (2x4x16 for 96 feet) are set perpendicular to the ground. (We know we are repetitive here but this feature is absolutely essential for a strong house.)

So now you have two layers of plastic (see Figure 9) - one for the top and resting on the top wires; one for the bottom set of wires and also resting on them. The top plastic and wires must be placed last. Place the inner layer first and tape or staple around the poles to get as tight a fit as you can. The best way to do this is to staple the inner plastic at one end of the house, then roll it to the first set of poles where you cut out enough to snugly fit each pole. Then go on to the next set where you repeat the process and continue on your way until you reach the other end of the house. Now put on the top wires and top plastic. When you study Figure 9, you will see that the inner top layer wires can be stretched tighter from time to time by using the turnbuckle. Because there may be some sag from time to time, it doesn't matter if the inner layer sags a little bit. As long as it drains good, it will be okay.

The top layer of wires is also adjustable. The twelve inch bolt and nut is adjustable from the outside - at the end of the house. This will do to some extent. But it is advisable to get the cheap inflation blower as soon as possible in order to keep the top layer of plastic from excessive rubbing against the wires. And, more importantly, to give more insulation from heat and cold.

In Figure 5, note the "direction of expansion". These houses will be connected to the right. If you want to go to the left, then reverse the procedure including the bed placement.

FIGURE 6: This shows bed placement - whether you use sand/gravel beds, tables or just place the plants in their pots on the ground. The inside floor area should have a cover of black plastic with two inches of sand on top. This will control weeds and help hold extra heat in the winter time. Drains have been drawn for sand/gravel bed culture. Use ordinary PVC piping. The beds for this purpose should drop about three inches for their entire length. Any kind of PVC drain will do - but do place a valve at the main outlet and do run the line away from the building, either to a pond or to water grass, etc.

This bed design allows for 1890 Square feet of growing area. This will give 1890 one gallon pots plenty of space for plant growth. Such a setup will make it easier to water with an ordinary garden hose and to fertilize by hand. This number of growing plants can quickly put you into business. Of course, seedlings will take up less space, but this is a good overall average to go by.

FIGURES 7,8,9: Figure 7 shows how to attach two houses, proceeding in the direction of expansion. Note "L" as detailed in Figure 8. The gutter along L should drop three inches in the 96 foot length. Figures 7,8,9 are self-explanatory. As a final word about plastic: the permanent plastic on the inside of the ends of the house and the outside should enclose all wood. But all the plastic must be so tied down that there is a continuous space throughout the roof, the sides and the ends. This is necessary in order to allow the inflation blower to function properly. In other words, when the sides are down and the house is closed, there will be an insulating envelope of air about the entire house.

Ways of starting out:

By using current prices for supplies and sales, all figures can be thoroughly documented to the point where it is possible to gain a net of $40,000 profit per year from 1/3 acre. This is the optimum size for a two-person operation. In the beginning not many hours will be required; but when the operation starts to get near the 1/3 acre size, the two people will both be working full-time. And the larger the operation grows, the less profit per unit area - because of energy and labor costs. It's possible for you to earn much more money if you choose to have your operation grow larger in size. Hydroponics can be a very profitable operation when handled correctly. Just how does an individual with limited funds get into this expensive but profitable business? As far as the author knows, no one has as yet tried to help this individual get his start. That's why this manual has been written and published. This manual can take an individual from "bare" ground and "empty" pocket to a greenhouse operation which can, possibly within three years, have him operating a full-scale, completely equipped, year-round greenhouse - all paid for out of profits as he goes.

When you're starting out a greenhouse is handy but not absolutely necessary. But let's look at one briefly. The average commercial greenhouse costs anywhere from $7.50 to $9.00 per sq ft when completed. With the greenhouse designed in this manual - a post-beam, taut-wire structure - you can erect a greenhouse sufficient unto your needs for about 52 cents per sq ft. If you add the heating/cooling package for year-round operation, you will need another 21 cents per sq ft (this amount being amortized over ten years).

Commercial houses will have tables and automatic feeding/watering - but a two-person beginning operation must do without this fancy stuff for the time being. You'll have to work a little harder but for $2.78 per sq ft you can have most of the advantages of sophisticated commercial setups. In addition, your greenhouse will be easier to heat and cool by utilizing low ceilings and ground solar absorption. The accompanying tables at the end of this chapter explain the costs and profit figures. As an aside here you can also do what some folks do in Oregon: place the greenhouse two feet down (or more) into the ground. Dig a ten inch trench all around the perimeter, place insulating foam on the outside rim, cheap plywood on the inside perimeter and pour with no-fines concrete. Use J bolts to attach your posts in the concrete. Then scoop out the dirt between the walls and allow for a system of drainage.

To repeat, whether you grow vegetables or potted plants you will want a black plastic "blanket" underneath - with about two inches of sand on top of it to keep out the weeds and to allow for solar absorption. Special plastic is available which is porous - it lets water through but no light. You must be careful of moisture collecting on the inside of the greenhouse - especially on the inner roof plastic. You don't want water dripping onto the plants, and you certainly want good drainage. This structure should withstand high winds if the posts have all been planted four feet into the ground. If you don't have the greenhouse funds in the beginning, even the 52 cents per sq ft, your profit "out in the open" can still pay for a that same greenhouse the coming fall.

This might possibly include the heating/cooling package which usually lasts for at least ten years and can be amortized over that period of time. You can also add the gutter system to one side of the first greenhouse and then build another house connected to the first. You keep adding more houses in the same fashion. Be sure to make space allowances for such expansion when you start up your first house. Plan the entire layout carefully.

The annual gross per sq ft of growing space in a commercial greenhouse (using potted plants, foliage for crops) should be in the neighborhood of $17-$25. You need a minimum of $12 per sq ft. This should give a net profit which may range from $5 to $8 per sq ft. **(ALL DOCUMENTATION IN THIS MANUAL IS BASED UPON SQ FT OF HOUSE AREA AND NUMBER OF POTS INVOLVED.)** Today's growers are adding movable carts and trays which can be squeezed together and give even more growing space! When you need aisle space, you can move these carts or trays apart.

So much for greenhouses. Suppose an individual comes along without that 52 cents per sq ft. What's he going to do? Plenty! He can grow out in the field under plastic and shade cloth, in beds or pots. (Growers do this in the Canary Islands; they do it in India; some are now doing it in America.) He can do everything in the field that he can do inside a greenhouse. And sometimes he can control the operation better. Adding the shade cloth to his 96' x 30' area, he can go through the summer because there are no sides to cut down the breezes. (During the first season, the sides are raised in the greenhouse proposed in this manual.)

Actually the greenhouse for the first year will be just about like the field application, except that the sides are pulled down during high winds and heavy rains. Some growers, especially those with the movable cart system, push their crops outside during good weather.

The individual's cost of growing will include pots, plastic covering (with splits in aisles areas for rain runoff) and shade cloth. The costs will be per pot: pot = .15, pot mix = .11, fertilizer = .01, tray = .06, water = .07, truck rental = .53, cuttings/seedlings = .23, shade cloth = .12, black plastic CT703 sheet = .09, clear plastic CT703 sheet = .09, 3" tip fencing posts and wire to hold up plastic = .04 for a total of $1.50 per pot. If he sells the potted plants wholesale for the normal average of $4.00 per pot, he will net at least $2.50 per pot. (We assume he has his own land and water supply. But if he has to lease or rent land and buy water, the figures will differ.)

Based upon the above figures and only two crops a year, he can clear $9450 for each 1890 sq ft of growing space. This is more than $40,000 per 1/3 acre! Theoretical? Perhaps. The grower will need to know what he's doing. And he will need some luck with the weather. In any case this wouldn't be the first time a grower has started in this manner - nor will it be the last. Besides, in many cases, most plants like to be outside, especially mums in the early spring. Mums like the air. They flower better when they are started in a field growing situation.

Now you can see how this individual would be able to start out on a "shoestring" - when compared to what he would have to invest otherwise. As with all businesses, he does have to invest something to get started. At least now he has a chance to get into the business.

Though this manual proposes potted plants and foliage for starting out - in order to get higher profits, this is not to say you can't do well in vegetable crops. Some growers do quite well with tomatoes and lettuce - if they have a year-round operation. Most only grow tomatoes from fall to spring - about nine months. And their product is so good that even when field-grown tomatoes from other regions of the country are selling at fair prices, the hydroponic tomatoes sell for much higher prices. These growers' success often depends upon their location. If your location is not the best, bear in mind it only costs 8-10 cents per pound to ship your crop to any point in the United States. Off-season prices can easily offset transportation costs. This manual recommends you sell your produce in areas as near your home as possible. The fresher the product the better.

Greenhouse structure and plastics:
As mentioned earlier, the toughest and most hail-resistant plastic this author has run across is sold by Northern Greenhouse Sales, Box 42, Neche, ND 58265. This material is unbelievable! Write for a sample and information. This plastic is woven or ribbed. It spreads the light. You never have any glare because the light is evenly distributed throughout the greenhouse. It's very hard to push a screw driver through this material - and much more difficult to make the hole any bigger once you do get the material punctured. This kind of cover should be very good for high snow and wind loads as well as hail storms. The distributors maintain this plastic is also cat proof! Other good plastic covers are: Polydress Sunsaver, Monsanto Cloud Nine and Lexan. Polydress Fog-Bloc is an additive used on plastic covers to prevent condensation and dripping inside the greenhouse.

Greenhouses should also allow for carbon dioxide enrichment, which will be discussed later. Dramatic increases in growth and flowering are found when carbon dioxide levels up to 2000 ppm (parts per million) are introduced during the daylight hours.

What is a good greenhouse? It doesn't necessarily have to be set up for hydroponics but it does have to be: easily cleaned and maintained, expandable without trouble, strong and adaptable to various crops, able to give the right environment for the crop being grown, can be converted to grow anything. **DON'T EVER BUY A TURNKEY SETUP WHICH IS DESIGNED FOR ONLY ONE OR TWO CROPS.** A strong greenhouse will be able to hold up heavy curtains and thermal blankets, can support a crop like tomatoes which are strung to its members. You will be able to add or take away equipment such as movable tables, watering systems, automatic controls.

Shop for your insurance - the rates will tell you which greenhouses are the better buys. Normally the higher the rate, the poorer the house. Sometimes cheaper is not better. Find out what the greenhouse environment will do to the superstructure. Acidic atmosphere, such as carbon dioxide, can attack zinc on galvanized members. Some metal structure greenhouse members can expand and contract a lot. This can cause misalignment. Today's commercially designed greenhouse also has overhead carriers or gantries. Load capacity will include the structure, everything attached to it or held by it, snow and wind pressures, overhanging baskets, and any other structure additions to hold plants.

The ideal cover should be cost effective, have good light transmission, be easily installed, hail resistant, fire retardant, and afford optimum plant growth. A ribbed or uneven surface design is better than a flat even surface. Colorless plastic which isn't extremely clear is best. The top cover or roof sheeting should be washed off with a hose at regular intervals. Don't overshade - use a light meter. If you use a shading compound, do so with two or three fine applications. Don't put it all on at one time. The further north your location, the lower the ceiling inside the house must be - especially for lettuce. Avoid too much glare - again, use a light meter. Lastly, find out the erection time when purchasing a greenhouse system. This will help in your planning - and your finances.

GREENHOUSE CONSTRUCTION
(Not drawn to scale)

FIGURE 1:

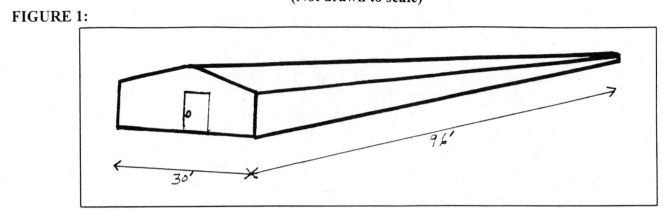

30'

96'

OVERALL VIEW

FIGURE 2:   SIDE VIEW:

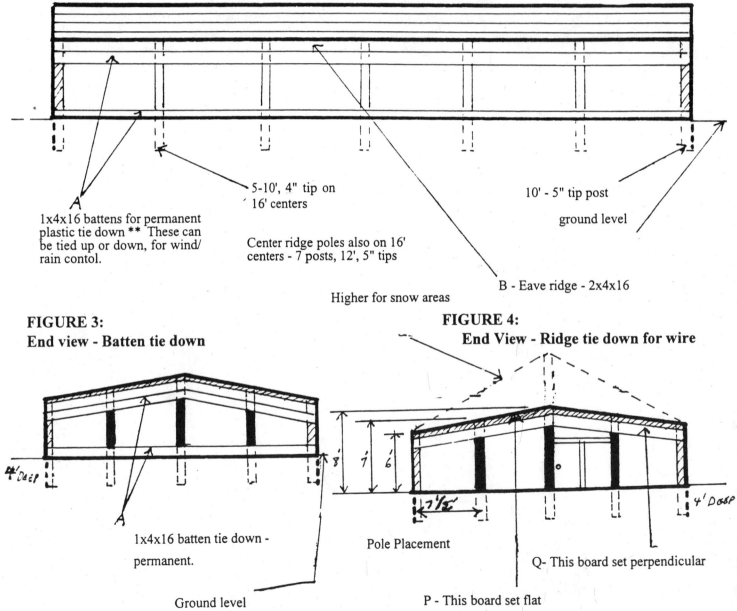

A

1x4x16 battens for permanent
plastic tie down ** These can
be tied up or down, for wind/
rain contol.

5-10', 4" tip on
16' centers

Center ridge poles also on 16'
centers - 7 posts, 12', 5" tips

Higher for snow areas

10' - 5" tip post

ground level

B - Eave ridge - 2x4x16

FIGURE 3:
End view - Batten tie down

4' Deep

A

1x4x16 batten tie down -
permanent.

Ground level

FIGURE 4:
End View - Ridge tie down for wire

8'   7'   6'

7½'

4' Deep

Pole Placement

Q- This board set perpendicular

P - This board set flat

76

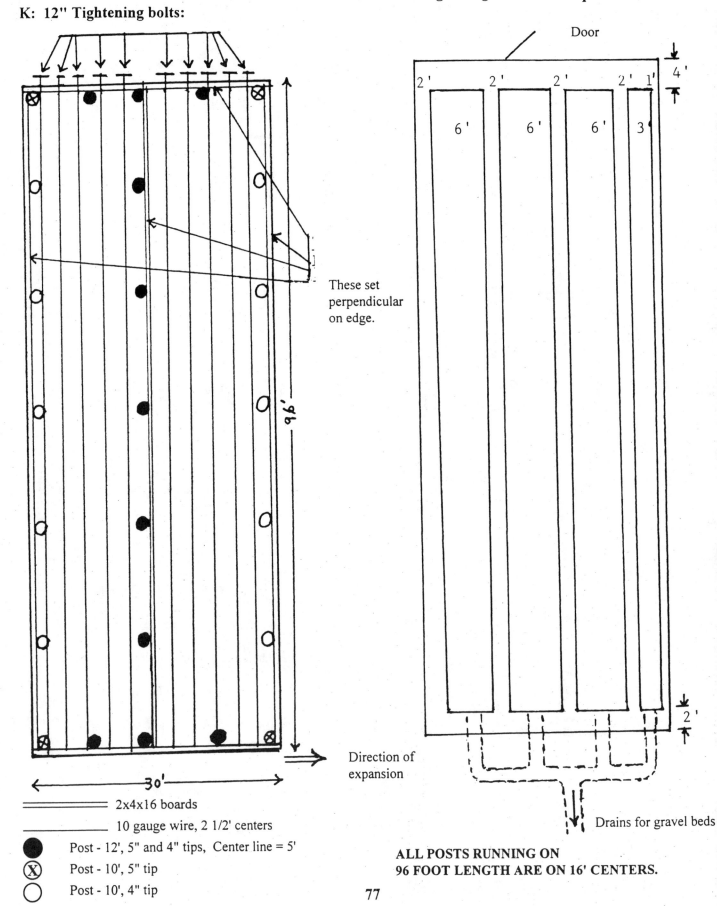

FIGURE 5:   TOP VIEW - Roof and Wire, beam, and post structure

K: 12" Tightening bolts:

These set perpendicular on edge.

96'

30'

Direction of expansion

≡≡≡ 2x4x16 boards

——— 10 gauge wire, 2 1/2' centers

● Post - 12', 5" and 4" tips, Center line = 5'

Ⓧ Post - 10', 5" tip

○ Post - 10', 4" tip

FIGURE 6:   TOP VIEW - Bed and aisle layout

Bed or growing area = 1890 sq ft

Door

4'

2'   2'   2'   2' 1'

6'   6'   6'   3

2'

Drains for gravel beds

ALL POSTS RUNNING ON 96 FOOT LENGTH ARE ON 16' CENTERS.

77

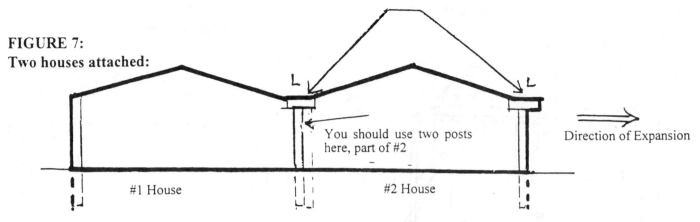

* Gutter and walkway -- End View

FIGURE 7:
Two houses attached:

You should use two posts
here, part of #2

Direction of Expansion

#1 House

#2 House

* Gutters and drainpipes should be at all edges (eaves) and lead to a tank or pond for future use. Of course, this is optional, but also wise.

FIGURE 8:   ""L"   Cross-section:

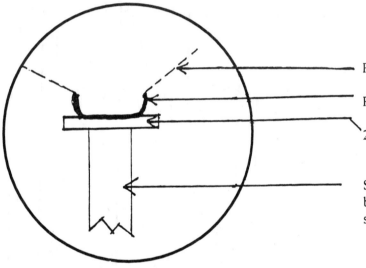

Plastic roof film

Plastic roofing attached here with clips or battens

2x12 walkway and support

Side post -- You may want to add a six foot support post between the regular side posts. A 2x12 should, however, be sufficient for a walkway.

FIGURE 9: "K" Cross-section:

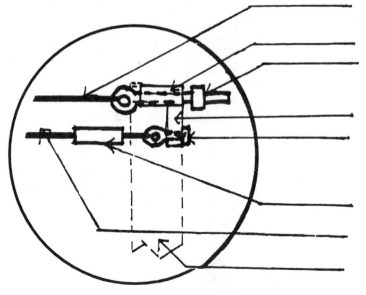

Monsanta 603 Mil Film on top here (Mil 6)

2x4x16 laid flat (to the ground)

12" eye bolt with nut and washer for <u>outside</u> tightening

2x4 laid perpendicular (to the ground)

eye bolt with lock nut. (The distance between wires should be about 4 inches.)

Turnbuckle for initial tightening.

Monsanta 603 Mil 4 Film on top here

End post.

Net profit per gal pot with wholesale price at $4.00 per pot:
*Options. (With operator doing all labor, not energy cost.)

Start At: Per Pot

A.   180 pots - plant directly into pot   .15   283.50   .15
      1/2 vermiculite, 1/2 peat moss
      1 gal pot = .09 cu ft
      1890 x .09 = 100 cu ft of mix
            50 cu ft vermiculite   4 cu ft = 7.89   98.63
            50 cu ft peat moss   5 cu ft = 11.40   114.00   .11

B.   Fertilizer (spread by hand)
      1 ounce/sq ft ever 7 - 10 days for three months (normally)
      1 gal pot - .15 sq ft top surface area
      1 ounce feeds 7 pots (just a pinch for each)
      10 feedings - 10 ounces/7 pots = 160# per crop.
      Using Peters 20-20-20   6.76 x 25#   19.63/25#   132.70   .07*
      Using Osmocote 14-14-14   3.38 x 50#   48.14/50#   162.71   .09*
      Using regular fertilizer at feed stores:
            12-24-12 or 13-13-13   3.38 x 50#   5.25/50#   17.75   .01

C.   Trays: 270   12 x 17 x 2   .41   110.70   .06*

D.   Water:
      Minimum 100 gal per pot (normally)
      City/rural - both must be tested before using
      and corrected if need be.   varies   varies   .07

E.   Cuttings:
      Seeds can be used but that would be a rather
      slow start; better to use cuttings.
      Average cost: .23   434.70   .23

F.   Greenhouse cost w/options 2 and 4:
      1330.03 + 173.85 + 441.00 + <u>2(217.32 + 144.89 + 173.85)</u> =
      3017.00 divided by 6 years = 502.83 divided by 2 crops =
      269.34/crop divided by 1890 =.13/pot/yr
      (Underlined is for plastic replacement in 3 yrs.)

G.   Truck rental and gas = $2,000/yr divided by 2 crops = 1000.00   .53
      Most contract orders are picked up or shipped via other lines.

ELECTRICITY AND PLUMBING? Not the first year! Electricity for water pump only.
Watering is done by hand and with a garden hose.

THIS PLAN ASSUMES YOU HAVE LAND AND WATER AVAILABLE.

H.   To add the complete heating/cooling packages: $6153.00
      Of course, this can be amortized over ten years and:
      6153 divided by 10 = 615.30   615.30 divided by 1890 =   .33*
      Add A, B, C, D E, F, G = $1.29 Min cost/pot   4.00 - 1.29 = 2.71 net profit
      Add above plus H = $1.62   4.00 - 1.62 = 2.38 net profit

Cost and materials for Greenhouse Frame and covering, ready to grow: 30 ft x 96 ft with 4 bed areas, 3 at 6 ft wide, 1 at 3 ft wide, 4 2 ft aisles. House area = 2880 sq ft; bed area = 1890 sq ft.

4 lbs nails	.90	3.60
10 side posts - 10', 4" tip	11.50	115.00
4 end posts - 10', 5" tips	11.50	46.00
7 center posts - 12', 5" tips	16.20	113.40
4 end posts - 11', 4" tips	16.20	64.80
1 roll (100#) 10 gauge wire	69.70	69.70
22 eye hooks	.30	6.60
10 eye hooks	.30	3.00
10 12" bolt and nut w/washer	2.19	21.90
11 turnbuckles	1.19	13.09
26 2x4x16 #2 YP	4.55	118.30
56 1x4x16 #2 YP	2.39	133.84
Lumber and hardware for doors	32.00	32.00
1 40x100' 603 Mil 6 (3 year) plastic	217.32	217.32
1 40x100' 603 Mil 4 (3 year) plastic	144.89	144.89
1 40x100' CT703 Mil 6 clear plastic	173.85	173.85
2 gal waterproofing for battens	11.97	23.94
24 stove bolts 1/4" x 6"	.30	7.20
48 hooks with eyes	.45	21.60 Sq Ft. Cost= .46
(1) Totals		1330.03

Interior options:

(2) Without gravel beds:
1 40' x 100' CT 703 black Mil 6 plastic, 3 year.	173.85	173.85	.06

(3) With gravel beds scooped from ground:
1 40' x 100' CT 703 black Mil 6	173.85		
52 cu/yds gravel/sand mix @14.00	728.00		
Mics for valves and PVC piping:	60.00	961.85	.33
(4) 36' x 100' 63% (+) shade cloth:	441.00		.12
(5) Entire heating/cooling package with plumbing	6153.00	6153.00	2.14

You can place five of these houses, interconnected, on 1/3 acre and have 120 sq ft left over.

Profit structure, using pot figures from page 79: 3780 pots at $2.38 profit each = $8,996.40. This times 5 houses = $44,982.00 for 1/3 acre! All figures are based on 8-1-93 prices. For inflation for years after 1993, and 2% per year. (From 1984-1992 inflation costs ran at this level.)
*NOTE: These figures are for growing directly on the ground - no trenches of any kind. Pots are set upon the ground with black plastic underneath.

CHAPTER 8

MORE ABOUT GREENHOUSES AND SOME SPECIFIC PROBLEMS:

Greenhouse and root-zone heating:

To conserve energy some growers have gone to split-night temperature control. This is done by reducing the air temperature for part of the night and using root-zone heating for the entire night. Most growers use root-zone heating entirely for the germination and seedling stage.

According to one authority, plants put on most of their growth during the first four hours of night. Therefor split-night temperature control is an idea for us to consider. An example of split-night temperature control would be to keep the air temperature at 60 degrees F for 4-6 hours and at 45 degrees F during the remaining night hours. Keep the root-zone temperature at 60 degrees F all night. Combining root-zone heating with split-night temperature control still needs some research to become more acceptable. Those with space and time may want to experiment with this idea. Remember that air temperatures below 45 degrees F cannot be offset by root-zone heating. Plants will slow down in growth below 45 degrees F. Some growers may rely too much on root-zone heating, especially during the winter months. As we have seen this reliance will not stand up when the air temperature is to low. You can't keep on raising root-zone heating without cooking the plants! So perimeter heating will be needed to help raise the air temperature.

Since a greenhouse is necessarily structured to be a very inefficient unit to heat and since energy costs are still one of our highest costs of doing business, a system for heating which has long been out of date is coming back into favor again. This is heating with hot water which entails a boiler or heater with valves, headers, autovents, pumps and necessary piping and hosing. Hot water heating still remains as our most efficient heat source. Hot water heating is expensive to install compared to other systems. But maintenance is much lower and the system will last a lot longer than others. When purchasing a hot water system you must first check what local and most likely available fuel is at hand. Then plan your boiler operation to accommodate that fuel. One authority suggests if you have a large area to heat, such as several greenhouses, that you should have several boilers or heaters. Just in case one goes out on a cold winter night.

Hot water heating has other advantages. You can create several mini-climates throughout the greenhouse and you heat the specific areas you want heated. You don't have to heat the entire greenhouse at the same temperature. And you don't need to heat non-productive areas. You can save up to 60% on energy costs as compared to other heating systems. But like any other equipment investment, the decision to use hot water heating is one which requires careful study and a supplier who knows exactly what he's doing. The system must be adapted to your current as well as your future needs. Here are some further thoughts on root-zone heating:

1. Part of efficient heat delivery will include using Foylon for root-zone heating. When placed beneath the root-zone heating equipment,this material will reflect any heat upward into the root and plant regions and save a lot on energy costs.

2. Thermal blankets are sometimes used in conjunction with root-zone heating. The blankets are hung directly above the plant canopies in order to trap the root-zone heat and make a small artificial atmosphere around the plants.
3. Root-zone heating should be kept at 100 BTUs per square foot. Any other temperature increases will have to be dealt with through perimeter heating.

Heating/cooling: Some tips for economy and use:

Unvented heaters are a way to lose plants. They may produce more heat but they also lose part of the crop. In addition some of these heaters produce carbon monoxide which is deadly to humans. Also produced are ethylene and oxides of nitrogen which are harmful to plants. If you are using one of these heaters in order to get carbon dioxide enrichment you must find a way to vent harmful gases. We are presently in the midst of a revolution in heating techniques and how we are to get warm air down to plant level. A lot of changes will be made in forced air gas heaters now used in upper and gable end areas of most greenhouses.

The size of heater you buy depends upon the following: total heat loss plus 10% for ventilation during winter months plus 10% for a location which is windy. To determine heat loss:

1. Add up the inside areas of all surfaces: the top, the two sides and the two ends.
2. For double glazed houses (two layers of plastic or glass all the way around), multiply the surface area found in 1 above by .80 and then multiply that by the daytime temperature at which you wish the crop to be grown. Single glazed houses should use a multiple of 1.25. These figures apply in general for areas near Latitudes 35-50 degrees.

This will give the heat loss in B.T.U.s (British Thermal Units) per hour. Now find a heater which will put out this amount of heat. The heater you choose should be able to put out this much heat to cover the losses - or a little greater to be on the safe side. Again, it's better to have two heaters to do the same job. In case one goes out, you will still have the safety factor of the remaining heater.

Some energy saving cooling techniques:
1. Shading: if you use a 70% shade effect, you can reduce your ventilation by 50%.
2. Evaporative cooling systems: Impurities in the water being used can be left behind on the pad and clog it. If you use a bleed off of 1 to 2% of the recirculating water, you can eliminate a lot of this. The impurities will appear as a frosty residue on the side of the fan which faces the outside.
3. Fans: If belt-driven, check to see if the belts are tight. The best way: 1/2 inch deflection at a distance 1/2 way between motor and fan. Replace the pulley with one the same size - not larger or smaller. If there is a worn shoulder in the V-groove, replace the pulley. Always run at recommended manufacturer's speed. Use the correct fan size for the greenhouse in question.
4. Natural cooling: Use side and roof ventilators. If possible, roll up the house walls.

Fan and Pad Method:

Plants such as tomatoes and cucumbers form a barrier which an cause a difference of 20 degrees in temperature from one end of the greenhouse to the other. Two hundred feet or less is the maximum length to try to move air. You need at least one air change per minute inside the greenhouse. Also you must keep in mind where the plants are located.

If you have a tubular air sleeve going down the ridge inside the greenhouse, you will find the temperature will fluctuate from one end to the other. If you have low lying plant stock, will the cooler air from the sleeve reach them? If you have one hundred feet or less in length to be cooled, you must figure everything differently. So it's really best to have the fan and pad and the entire cooling system computed by the manufacturer's engineers. Don't forget to check other competitive systems before buying. Allow pads to dry out between crops or when needed. At present Aspen excelsior is used in pads. A paper pad is out from Mintors Company of Florida, but it though superior to Aspen excelsior is quite expensive. The paper pad has a life of nearly ten years if properly tended.

How to save energy:

Although it isn't desirable to make a greenhouse completely air-tight, there is still much you can do to help decrease your energy costs.

Probably the most effective technique would be to insulate the north wall of your greenhouse. Since little light will come from that quarter, you can insulate by using a 1 inch board of foil-covered polyurathane foam. This has the insulating qualities of 3 1/2 times the double inflated polythene walls which no doubt you already have. By themselves the double layers of plastic can save you over 40% heat loss as compared to a single layer.

With some crops you can reduce the temperature inside your growing area. A five per cent temperature decrease gives anywhere from 20-35% savings in heat required. But you can't do this unless you maintain good practice in plant cultivation. Now's the time also to check your thermostats. Those which don't work properly can rob your heating/cooling apparatus by decreasing the overall efficiency. Thermostats should be accurately calibrated at least once a year. And they should be placed where they can do the most good. A thermostat should not be in line with air flow from fans or heaters. They should also be covered to keep the sun from having any effect. The best location for a thermostat is usually at plant level in the center of the greenhouse. A thermostat should not be attached to a wall. Finally, if you're using an aspirate thermostat (one which pulls air over the sensor), you should place it where the air will be pulled over the sensor and not blown upon it.

Horizontal air flow is also important. Especially after the ventilating fans have been turned off. In order to prevent air stratification, it's smart to place fans at various locations around the greenhouse. They should all blow together and form a circular air movement around the greenhouse interior. The fan velocity should be at least 40 feet per minute. You can check how the air is moving by placing strips of paper on 2 foot stakes at certain intervals. When all the strips are fluttering in the breeze, you know you have the proper air movement.

For a 30 x 100 ft house place two fans (each capable of moving 700 cu ft/minute), one on each side of the house about midway and next to a wall. Each fan should be blowing in the opposite direction from its companion. This air circulation will mix the air inside the house and cut down the incidence of disease. Ventilation fans should be attached to the leeward side of the house. In this way they can get help from the prevailing winds. You must place them where they won't interfere with nearby structures, particularly other greenhouses.

Weatherstripping around doors can be very important. A 1/2 inch crack can cost over $100 a year! A good guide is this: to replace any lost carbon dioxide, a one inch square opening for every 2000 BTUs your inside furnace puts out will be sufficient. Again, make certain all harmful fumes are properly exhausted to the outside. One more thing: you might consider other kinds of fuel. Wood is supposed to be the cheapest and most cost-effective. But a lot of growers say it's too much mess and too much work. If you're using wood to fire a hot water heating system, you could get a full payback on the system within two years.

Blanketing: How to save energy costs in a very simple way:

The environmental factors necessary for plant growth are: the air temperature, its humidity, it velocity, its gaseous percentages. In addition to these we have to consider the media: its temperature, its humidity, its gas percentages, its chemical balances. Finally, both visible and invisible radiation must be considered.

Blankets or "energy curtains" are a method for controlling radiation and energy gain or loss. Although white washes can be used on the outside roof of the greenhouse, it is better to use fabric shading inside the greenhouse in order to control the amount of shading. By using light meters you won't make the mistake of too much or too little shading. You must select you shading fabric with care as different fabrics respond with different results. The amount of radiation from the sun which reaches the plant will depend not only on the greenhouse cover but also on the type of shading you use. A proper fabric blanket can reduce heat needs at night by at least 50%.

You use shading during daylight to cut down on excess sunshine, depending on the crop you're growing. You also use it at night. especially during the winter months, to cut down on heat loss. In either case, your blanket will be a thin fabric which can be pulled out over polypropolyne monofilament line. You can pull either from side to side or from one end of the greenhouse to the other. The fabric must be the kind which will fold easily upon itself when not in use. It can then be packed against the eave on one side or at the north end if used lengthwise in the greenhouse. Your apparatus for this should be a system where the fabric can be pulled into a horizontal position above the crop - usually at the height of the eave (or gutter) of the house. You can either move the blanket by hand or have it automated.

What type of fabric should you use?

That depends upon the crop. Generally porous materials are best because water doesn't collect or condense on top and make the blanket difficult to handle. However, solid fabrics give more insulating qualities and thus save more energy. In most cases the fabric should be porous, strong, easy to handle, low in cost, capable of good insulation and high light reflection. Many growers settle for a white porous fabric which shades by 50%. They do this during the summer because it makes the greenhouse climate easier for workers to work in. By using blanketing in this manner, some of your fans can be reduced in size and number - by 25-35%. But if you select the fabric based only on summer readings, you will lose some energy savings later on. A certain compromise must be made between summer and winter shadings.

We have seen some growers who use shade cloth on the outside roof of the greenhouse. **THIS PRACTICE IS NOT RECOMMENDED** because the fabric will collect dirt and cut down on the amount of light being transmitted to the crop. Also the fabric will weather and wear out much faster. No doubt the rising cost of fabric will slow down and eliminate this practice. Vertical curtains can be used - especially at night and during the winter months. These curtains can be either porous or solid but solid will give more protection from heat loss. Since the curtain is vertical, you don't have to worry about condensation. The curtains are placed vertically right next to the crop. Some growers will even move the crop close together on wintry nights and "box in" the crop with vertical curtains on all four sides. Then they will use the overhead blanket to prevent upward radiation.

Humidity control in greenhouses:

There are basically two ways to control humidity and disease in greenhouses. The first is selecting the right fan or fans and the consequent ventilator openings. The second is bringing in outside air (if the humidity of the outside air is lower) and using extra heating. Because of the tightness of modern greenhouses, humidity and carbon dioxide control are important profit-making tools. First let's talk again about fans. You must make sure the design is correct for your fans and your ventilator inlets. Control isn't as important for cold weather periods as it is for periods of hot weather. During cold weather the warm moist air inside a greenhouse rises and vents itself through the roof vents.

Because of their low cost, high volume propeller fans which give low pressure are commonly used in greenhouses. For economical reasons we must design our ventilating systems to accept this low-cost propeller which should deliver 18,000 to 20,000 cu ft per minute for every horsepower used when at a static water pressure of 0.10 inches. To do so we must have vents which thoroughly mix both outgoing and incoming air. This mixing will give uniform temperatures throughout the greenhouse and won't chill those plants sitting near the inlets. This also means keeping doors and other openings shut when the fans are in use.

To get the proper vent size, divide by 700 the cubic feet of air being delivered by the fan/fans. This may result in a vent or vents which are long and narrow and which are placed opposite the fan/fans. What happens then is the incoming cooler air is thoroughly mixed with the warmer air inside the greenhouse.

Another method of controlling humidity is by removing the excess humidity by bringing in outside air which has a lower humidity. It may be raining outside. Evenso, if the outside temperature is significantly lower than the greenhouse temperature, then you can pull in that outside air with a fan. You then heat that air to the proper temperature to gain over-all control of humidity inside the house. If you simultaneously exhaust a given amount of air and then replace it with cooler air from outside which can be heated and thus lower its relative humidity, you gain a lower humidity for the entire greenhouse. Lower humidity - at least down to 65-70% - will prevent fungus attacks such as Botrytis and powdery mildews. Preventing these will save labor costs and give more marketable fruits and plants.

Carbon dioxide enrichment:

Plants and flowers will grow much faster with carbon dioxide enrichment. This gas should be added during daylight hours and often can be used in conjunction with a heating device. In other words, you can enrich and heat at the same time. But why do it at all? Carbon dioxide is necessary for photosynthesis. Plants won't grow without it. Since our object is to **RAISE BOUNTIFUL CROPS AS QUICKLY AS POSSIBLE**, anything extra we can do to make this happen is worthwhile.

Plants inside a greenhouse will quickly use up the normal availability of carbon dioxide which is usually .03% of air volume or 300 parts per million. When this happens the plants do not grow. They just sit there and maintain the status quo. This can happen when weather conditions make you close the vents and restrict the outside-inside interchange of air. Since hydroponics doesn't use soil, another source of carbon dioxide is lost. Therefor to keep normal carbon dioxide supplies on hand you must either have good ventilation and/or add more carbon dioxide.

Plants will respond dramatically to extra carbon dioxide. The recommended extra amount is between 800-1600 ppm (parts per million). This can be supplied with heaters if you have them vented properly and if you know how much carbon dioxide they put out. Also carbon dioxide can be supplied by special generators or even bottled carbon dioxide. Which method you choose will depend upon cost. **CAUTION: DO NOT GO ABOVE 2000 PPM** as this will be toxic to the plants! Above 4000 ppm will be toxic to you! Keep in mind that carbon dioxide is heavier than air. It will flow downward!

Other methods for getting carbon dioxide enrichment are from organic materials and dry ice. These are impractical and are not recommended unless you are growing on a very small scale. **ANOTHER CAUTION:** Methane gas is created by organic decomposition. It is deadly and must be vented outside.

Carbon dioxide from heaters:

If the flame of the fuel you are using is blue or colorless, you are generating carbon dioxide. If the flame is yellow or red, you are generating carbon monoxide which is deadly to both plants and animals. Fuels which burn with a blue flame are natural gas, butane, propane and alcohol. Heaters give off heat! So if you're using this method in the summer months you will have to vent the heat outside. Normally this method is mostly used during the winter months when the extra heat and growth are welcome. Regardless of what method you use, carbon dioxide enrichment must be done inside a SEALED greenhouse. If the vents are open, you are wasting money. You will need a re-circulating fan to keep the carbon dioxide moving around inside the greenhouse.

Plants will need more water and nutrient if they get extra carbon dioxide. To keep the carbon dioxide at the right level, you will have to know the interior volume of the greenhouse. If you are buying a generator from your supplier, he should be able to help work out the necessary figures for you. Bear in mind that even in a "tightly" closed greenhouse, there are sufficient leaks to make a 100% air exchange between outside and inside every 2 hours! Also keep in mind you will have to use more carbon dioxide when there is more light than usual.

Bottled carbon dioxide:
This is becoming more popular because you can control it more easily and accurately. You will have to check with the supplier to make certain you have the correct mechanical setup. This system entails piping, a regulator valve, a solenoid valve, a flow meter and a timer.

Most depletion of carbon dioxide occurs in greenhouses north of latitude 38 degrees. During the cooler months, growers in this area will tend to seal off the greenhouse and thereby cut off carbon dioxide from the outside. These growers need to enrich their greenhouses with carbon dioxide.

Adding carbon dioxide also gives plants longer shelf life. The optimum carbon dioxide level is 1000 ppm. One cubic yard of natural gas equals one cubic yard of carbon dioxide. A greenhouse which is fully cropped will need 625 cubic feet of natural gas per hour per acre to have 1500 ppm maintained carbon dioxide level. You also have to watch for the sulphur content in the fuel you use. Sulphur gas is toxic to plants. Carbon dioxide enrichment is needed on both dark and sunny winter days. Continuous (as opposed to sporadic) carbon dioxide enrichment seems to give the best results, according to Norwegian growers. Generally the Norwegian growers recommend carbon dioxide enrichment at 800-1000 ppm. They recommend pure carbon dioxide from bottles or other industrial containers. They also insist you should always check for ethylene in the source you use.

Carbon dioxide is especially beneficial under low light conditions such as in winter and on cloudy days. Carbon dioxide enrichment gives you stronger and taller seedlings, root systems which are more extensive, and substantially larger leaf areas. You get faster maturity and higher crop yields. For lettuce this can give an additional crop per year. Tomatoes and cucumbers show favorable response also. Sounds like more of this would be the right thing to do? Not so. As stated before, when you go over 1000 ppm you don't gain any benefits. You lose money, and you may lose the crop. This is a case of too much of a good thing.

Carbon dioxide deficiency may show up in plants which seem to grow too slow, which look poor and which stretch. How can you make certain your plants are getting enough carbon dioxide? First you need to know how much carbon dioxide is already present inside the greenhouse. For this you need a measuring device. You need a device which you can leave for 24 hours a day inside the greenhouse. This device should also be attached to an alarm. Carbon dioxide is usually added at night between sunset and sunrise. If you decide to use other sources of carbon dioxide rather than liquid, you must exercise care. Specifically, you will need a carbon monoxide alarm also installed within the greenhouse. If you're using natural gas or kerosene burners to furnish carbon dioxide, it's a good idea to shut them off at night. Burners should also have some sort of device (usually infra-red) which analyzes gases emitted by fuel burners and determines how much carbon dioxide is being emitted and which keeps the burners in line with the desired carbon dioxide concentration.

Further ideas which may be put to use:
- Single spanned greenhouses, if they are large, are more efficient than multi-spanned.
- The proper slope for greenhouses in the United States is between 26 degrees and 32 degrees. This range provides the most light entry. It also allows snow to slide off and prevents condensation from collecting on the inner roof.
- Wetting down greenhouse aisleways in the summer is not recommended. Better to use evaporative cooling or introduce a fine mist by mechanical means.
- Use evaporative cooling to get the highest efficiency. Make sure the pads have no breaks in them and are continuous. They must be wet or else hot spots will occur and reduce efficiency by letting hot air in.
- Want more efficiency? Consider the following. Store materials where they'll be handy. Keep everything including plant tags clearly marked. Standardize your containers and consider limiting them to just a few sizes. Use a prepared mix. Use pre-filled containers or fill containers during slack periods and stack on a pallet and cover with plastic to keep in the moisture. Make a movable potting bench. Then pot and place on the growing bench as you move from one end of the greenhouse to the other. Have extra money? Think about an overhead conveyer for moving filled flats/pots to their various growing areas.
- Labor costs can be cut by eliminating long walkways, by planting at one end and harvesting at the other, by using better cultivars, by using extra artificial lighting in the seedling phase, and by having work done at waist-high level.
- Do you have good air circulation in your greenhouse? If the leaves of all the plants in your greenhouse aren't gently moving - like in a spring breeze, then you don't have enough air circulation! Plastic air jet tubes are available to correct poor circulation. You may have seen a large plastic tube running down the top center of a greenhouse. This is used for heating and cooling. And this is not what we're talking about. It's better to have plastic tubes of a smaller nature connected to a large fan (able to keep all tubes inflated at the same time). Lay the tubes along the aisles and under the benches and along the walls. Puncture or make slits in the tubes where you want air to come out. This way all plants will benefit from constant circulation.
- Windbreaks can save up to 16% of winter heating costs. Plant (or tree) windbreaks are cheaper and just as effective as fence windbreaks.
- Unit costs is what it's all about. Though it's important to save on energy, sometimes it's more profitable to accelerate heating and produce plants faster.

- According to one authority, American growers are in a very good position. Why? Retail floral outlets are expanding so fast that within the next few years there won't be enough growers to satisfy the demand.
- Other factors to consider when buying greenhouse covers: light transmission, cost, control of condensation, flammability, durability and energy efficiency.
- Some West Canadian growers recommend Durafilm 3. At 6 mil thickness it will last for nearly 7 years in British Columbia and 6 years in the Yukon. Contact suppliers in that area.
- Some polythene films now being produced have antifog additives. This helps prevent dripping from the interior roof.
- In planning a greenhouse layout, efficiency is the catchword. Efficiency in plant and personnel movement. Efficiency in transplanting and shipping. Everything must come under the head of efficiency. Clear bay structures are needed for equipment to be moved easily and quickly. Sometimes it's better to have gutter-connected greenhouses (with the headhouse at one end) in order to get the efficiency one wants. Single small greenhouses have their place but they're not necessarily efficient and profitable. More heating/cooling is needed for small greenhouses standing by themselves. Also plants and employees are continually going in and out.

Other items to consider:
- Check ground water levels in the area in which you propose to build. You may have to lay tile for drainage or bull-doze the site to a higher level. You should install swales around the outside of the greenhouse to direct drainage away from the site. (1 inch of rain = 26,000 gallons of water per acre!)
- Construction next to a highway is important - for shipping and for customer and employee access. Support buildings should be built and organized around the central growing area. Everything should flow with a minimum of cross traffic and handling.

CHAPTER 9

VARIOUS HYDROPONIC GROWING TECHNIQUES

Nutrient film technique: Sometimes called nutrient flow technique.

This is the only new technique in hydroponics in forty years. It was introduced in the late sixties by Dr Allan Cooper of England. Basically, you recirculate a small quantity of nutrient in or down a trough or gully in which the roots of a plant are allowed to stand. The trough or gully is made of polythene plastic or a fixture lined with plastic. If plastic is used alone it is formed like a triangle. The plants are inserted every few inches and at prescribed intervals. The plastic is then drawn up around the plants and closed to keep out the light.

Labor costs are reduced by avoiding long walkways and having the operation at waist level. In the beginning you can grow on the floor, providing you have an even slope all the way for your gutter or trough. One successful family in Holland has their entire greenhouse floor cast in concrete, with gutters pre-cast in the concrete! But we wouldn't suggest your going that far. The troughs should not be longer than 60-65 feet; otherwise the plants at the far end will not get enough nutrient. Most growers now allow the trough to be only 30 feet long and placed perpendicular to a central collecting trough which runs the length of the greenhouse.

Roughly the suggested width and depth for tomatoes is 8 x 4 inches; for cucumbers: 10 x 4 inches; for lettuce: 3 x 1 inches. Today's growers have installed an aeration device at the tap where the nutrient goes into the trough. This provides ample oxygen and prevents root rot. The troughs must be even to prevent pooling at low spots and thereby causing root rot. Rate of descent is 1-2% or 12 inches drop per 100 feet, 6 inches drop per 50 feet. The flow rate of the nutrient is 1/4 to 1/2 gallon per minute for each trough. Depth of the nutrient is about 1/2 inch at all times during the growth of the plants. If necessary, more aeration at the tap source can enable you to keep the nutrient at a higher level. Just be certain the nutrient gets to all the plants and their roots - all the way down the line.

Capillary matting in Ariel NFT:

This technique uses a "W" shaped trough. The trough is lined with plastic and capillary matting is laid on the center ridge and its sides. The plant is centered on the ridge (pockets hold it in place) - then half the roots are allowed to trail down one side of the ridge and half down the other side. Nutrient solution is allowed to flow down one gully for a while, and then down the other gully for a while. This method insures the plant gets proper amounts of air and nutrient.

Following the diagram given here, plant C is anchored to center ridge of "W" shaped trough. Capillary matting lies on both sides of the center ridge and draws nutrient from gullies A or B to the plant roots, now half way down the A and B sides. Roots don't clog the floor of the trough and they get ample air and nutrition. The entire top plastic is pulled up around the plant and closed.

Nutrient uptake controls are advised for the beginner. It is believed that plants don't always pick up what they need from the nutrient solution. It is also believed that Ariel NFT will replace the older NFT methods - that only bare-root plants will be used and no solid media such as rockwool cubes will be used. There will be less root clogging and root rot. Systems will be much simpler with less control and monitoring. More attention will be directed to increasing plant nutrition and better tasting fruit.

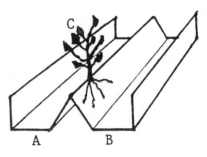

Hypertonic feeding:

This is another concept introduced by Dr Cooper and his associates. A significantly higher concentration of nutrients is allowed to flow through the NFT system - at a time when leaf transpiration is at its highest (most light of the day coming in). After about thirty minutes, the original solution is allowed to flow again through the system. Results: higher fruiting and production.

Use of ultra-violet light:

Most growers in the United States use ultra-violet lamps at the return end of the solution pipe - to kill any bacteria or fungus which may have gained access to the system. However you must check the system frequently because ultra-violet light will precipitate iron by 100% and boron and manganese by 20% within a 24 hour period. You will have to use extra iron through foliar feeding. Spraying a feeding solution directly on the leaves of a plant is called foliar feeding. It also helps to keep the ultra-violet light bulb clean.

Other things to keep in mind: Pump failure is number one. This is why the catchment tank must be large enough to hold all the fluid in the system - in case there is a pump or electrical failure. Secondary pumps and extra power units should be kept available in case of such failures. The nutrient must be kept flowing without interruption. Controls must be maintained for pH, nutrient mix and electrical conductivity (E.C.). These controls are attached to injector systems which draw in materials as needed. Some growers replace the entire nutrient mix only once a month. But with the help of computers in more sophisticated commercial installations, nutrient control and other supplementation is done on a daily, sometimes hourly, basis.

One authority believes the root system of a growing plant must have continual access to air which has a minimum oxygen content of 21%. Systems which do not restrict nutrient flow or where roots do not clog up the system are considered to be superior to other systems. These systems not only would include NFT but also Ein-Gedi and the Skaife method.

Root death comes at times of great stress, such as fruiting time. If most of the roots are white, don't worry about root death. Controlling pythium, a major fungus disease, is done by keeping the nutrient solution between 68 and 77 degrees F. Sometimes the nutrient solution can vary greatly without harm to the plants. **WHAT CANNOT BE VARIED IS THE RATIO OF THE VARIOUS ELEMENTS TO EACH OTHER WITHIN THE GIVEN SOLUTION.** (These ratios are given in the fertilizer formulations in the first section.)

NFT techniques in the Third World: or how to teach Hi-Tech to the natives.

Dr Cooper believes NFT technology transfer needs to be done in the underdeveloped Third World countries. But how do you teach uneducated natives to produce food with the high-tech methodology of NFT? To do so properly might take a hundred years. Meanwhile the Third World becomes hostage to more uncomfortable political ideologies. Dr Cooper believes the problem is not technical. Rather the problem is economic, social and political. No one seems to want the problem solved - not even the people who are mostly concerned. Dr Cooper's Ariel Industries of England has come up with what he believes to be the solution. He proposes support centers for NFT growers in a given area.

Here's how a support center would work. Establish a small staff (say two experts in NFT technique) in an area where you have potential growers. Depending upon the crops being grown, these two people would visit on a regular basis and sample nutrients being used in a grower's NFT system. This information would be analyzed and fed through a computer at the support center. A fertilizer formulation for a definite period of time and designed for the crop being grown would be put together and sent to the grower involved. The grower needn't know what's in the formulation; he needn't know all the complexities or for that matter any of them.

The most effort the grower would put out, aside from setting up the NFT system (with support center help), would be to take two hours of training at the outset. During this period of time he would be taught how to use two simple instruments. For example, every morning he puts a dip stick (which changes color) into the head tank of his system. The color on the stick when matched with a color chart he has on hand tells him exactly what to do. Each color designates "buckets" full of acid. If the color he gets on the stick says to add three buckets of acid, then that's all he has to do. He doesn't have to know how to mix the acid or what's in it. All he has to do is to place the dip stick and add the required acid. Thus he keeps the pH of the system under control.

The other instrument is a hand meter which measures electrical conductivity. Mind you he doesn't have to know what this instrument is all about. All the grower has to do is take some of the nutrient from the head tank and place it in the meter. The subsequent reading will tell him how many buckets of fertilizer he needs to bring his nutrient solution up to par. That's all there is to it! Anyone could do it. And probably with more success than most of us do everyday with our own methods.

It is believed that NFT could also be done just as well in the open as under plastic and inside. In fact it is believed that NFT could be the saving grace of the future. What with hypertonic feeding, crops can be brought in which fall within the size and quality guidelines which supermarket chains are beginning to expect as the norm. Hypertonic feeding can also offset the lesser percentage of light transmission which plastic has as opposed to glass.

Aeroponics:

A variation of the Israeli Ein-Gedi method may be in our future. This system is still in the developmental stage. But it follows good precepts and is worth looking at if only because it's simple to operate and doesn't need a lot of machinery. The idea as explained in the figure of the BOX was developed by Cabot Laboratories, Petersham, Ma. The ideal really goes back all the way to 1950 when it was proposed by Went's Earhart Laboratories in Pasadena, CA.

Explanation of the BOX: Box F is lined with white or black plastic (E). The box can be made of plywood. The plastic should be in two layers of 4 mil each. The top of the box (G) is covered with plastic "egg crating" (Fluorescent screen). This should be of a strong variety with compartments of 1.27 cm squared. On top of this lay a 4 mil sheet of black plastic and on top of that a sheet of aluminum foil to reflect heat away from the box. Holes are regularly spaced for the plants (D). Cut right through the plastic and stick in the plant. Don't put the roots any closer to the motor than 25 cm - this is to make sure the roots get plenty of spray.

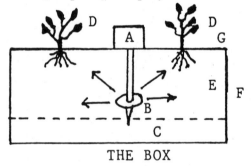

THE BOX

The motor (A) should be raised above the box in order not to vibrate the plants. This can be done with two vertical side boards and one top horizontal board. The spinner (B) is the type you find in humidifiers. For further information contact Northern Electric Co, P O Box 469, Waynesboro, MS 39367. You'll need a motor which can work for long periods of time while in a vertical position. You can get one from Bodine Electric Co, Chicago, IL. Such a motor should be rated: 1-1.5 hp with rpm of 3450 and which can run on 0.6 amp and regular 115 voltage. The spinning shaft should be stainless steel. The tip of the spinner should be immersed 1 1/4 to 2 cm into the nutrient solution (C). When the motor is running, the nutrient will run up to the spinner and be flung off in a fine mist in all directions. You must maintain the depth of the spinner tip at 1 1/4 to 2 cm at all times. Since the tip has a tendency to clog, you'll have to clean it at intervals. Both of these difficulties can be management problems. Engineering might be able to solve the first. The second may become labor intensive.

Here you have a system which is very simple, efficient, and very correct for plants. Roots have no chance to clog the system as they might in NFT. They are continually being fed and aerated under the healthiest conditions possible. Chances of disease and infection are dramatically reduced. Opportunities for optimum growth are at the maximum. And two prime conditions are satisfied: plenty of air, plenty of nutrient. Whether or not this idea is commercially feasible remains to be seen. The idea is still in its infancy and may only prove to be useful to the hobbyist or the scientific grower. The Ein-Gedi system of aeroponics (misting) is very successful in Israel and in some commercial installations in the United States. But a misting idea using spinners and motors will require a lot of intensive research to make it work commercially. The motors alone constitute a major hurdle. Still one noted authority thinks this is the only way to go. Most certainly it's the purist's way to go.

AVRDC: A new hydroponic system from the tropics:

AVRDC or non-circulating hydroponics is a system now being tried out in some tropical regions where soils are notoriously deplete of nutrients and where insects, heat and moisture abound. The system was developed in Taiwan and designed for untrained personnel. It has the following advantages over NFT and other current hydroponic systems in use. The daily need for adjusting pH, EC, nutrient and oxygen is eliminated. Plus the higher startup costs for most recent systems are also dramatically reduced. Those are the claims made for AVRDC. Judge for yourself. The principle is similar to one which was used when the author was doing organic gardening. Although the author didn't know about AVRDC at the time, he did suspect the reason he did so well with his intensively grown raised beds was because the root systems of his plants never got to the point where they became waterlogged. Essentially this is the way AVRDC works.

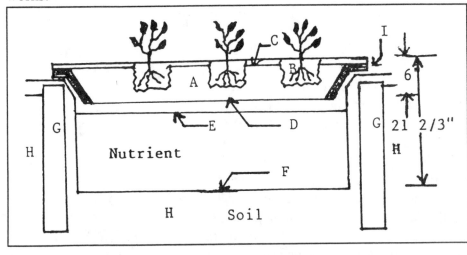

In the drawing, seedling bags (B), filled with perlite, are anchored in a (C) polythene cover which fits on top of (I) a wooden rack with side of polythene and a bottom (D) of nylon netting which measures 3 x 2.5 cm in mesh dimension. The size of the wooden rack with polythene sides and net bottom depends upon how wide a growing box you use. In the tropics they usually place this unit in the ground to keep the nutrient solution cool. There is no reason why this couldn't be done in our climate. Except for one thing: the earth is an enormous heat sink. During the winter months the ground can get too cold. In the tropics growers would have (G) concrete container walls set into the ground. Clay walls or brick would do just as well. Container walls can also be built above ground but at a higher cost. (H) represents soil.

(A) in the drawing represents air space, (D) is the netting on the bottom of the wooden rack, (E) is the nutrient level which is normally kept constant, (F) is .3 mil (or thicker) plastic film for the lining. The .3 mil size will last for about a year in the tropics.

The principle works like this: the seedling is already thoroughly rooted in the bag before insertion into the top polythene cover. The seedling immediately begins to develop roots in the moist air space between the cover and the nutrient solution. Most of the roots when hitting the netting below will branch out and form a matting of (Oxygen) roots above the netting. Other roots will go through the netting and into the nutrient solution for no more than six inches. They are called W (Water) and N (Nutrient) roots. The results are excellent growth because the plant is always getting plenty of oxygen as well as water and nutrients. What's more, the plant doesn't take up as much nutrient because it doesn't have to waste energy in growing long nutrient and water roots. Only three things have to be tended to; keep the nutrient/water level at the same height (this can be done with a ball valve), have access to air replenishment for (A) air space shown in drawing, and (in the tropics) have the entire affair enclosed inside a net house to keep out injurious insects.

Why the seedling bag? Aside from offering additional support for the plant the bag helps prevent heat stress during the hot months. The seedling in its bag isn't placed in the top cover (C) until the seedling's roots are starting to come out of the bag. At this stage your water/nutrient level should be set 2 to 4 inches above the netting to help get the seedling's roots growing. The level should be gradually lowered (depending on root growth) to about 1-2 cm under the net and kept that way until harvest time. Thus all three types of roots (O,W,N) will be able to develop.

The success for this system depends upon how fast the O roots develop. Fertilizer is normally replenished every three weeks, depending on the crop. Locally available fertilizers are used. You can use the same fertilizer solution for various crops, like tomatoes, cucumbers and lettuce, if they have similar needs. The smaller the container used the more frequently you need to replenish the fertilizer. If you use a container which holds more than 330 gallons of nutrient solution, you will fertilize less often - three weeks after transplanting and every two weeks thereafter until harvest. Except for during the hot months, seedlings are sprouted in vermiculite or perlite and then transplanted directly through holes in the cover (C). A roofing of plastic is used over the housing with the insect netting at the sides.

Flood benches: Or flood and ebb:

A flood bench is one with a plastic top on which you can set potted plants. The entire bench top is like a large pan into which you can flood your nutrient and/or water to a certain level. After the plants have picked up ample moisture from the flood around them, you can allow the fluid to drain off and into a storage tank from which you can pump again at regular intervals. Most growers who use this method believe it saves time and labor as well as water and fertilizer. The Japanese like it very much.

Thinking of installing this system? Consider the following first. Don't pot on the flooding benches - waste will get into your storage tank. Don't push flats or pots across the plastic top - you will scratch and make a leak for the next flooding. Have benches which can be leveled in every direction. Always know the EC (Electrical Conductivity) and the pH of your medium and your irrigating or flood water. Keep all test instruments clean and test at least once a week. And have benches which are very sturdy - water can be heavy stuff.

Aquaculture: Growing plants and fish together:

Although the raising of fish in ponds is an idea which is more than 2,000 years old, the raising of plants and fish together has not been, to date, a successful enterprise. The Chinese in their ancient rice paddies did bring plants and fish together in a modified form and they still do so today. By raising various kinds of carp and letting the water flow out of the pond into sluiceways planted with water hyacinths, the Chinese managed to purify the pond water and to increase the hyacinth crop. The water hyacinths were harvested and used as a compost for other crops.

Raising fish in ponds has become a foremost industry in many parts of the world, not only in Asia and Europe but also in America where cat fish ponds abound in the South. Trout farms are also prevalent in America. But putting crops like tomatoes and lettuce together with fish is still in its infancy. Research in the United States has recently directed attention to small carefully controlled systems which incorporate plants and fish. Several methods have ben proposed, including a tank with plants floating in a styrofoam sheet. The roots of the plants are protected from the fish by wire netting. A space above the netting is provided where the roots can have access to air (see AVRDC). The main part of the plant's root system dangles in the water and is able to absorb as much as 28% of the excess nitrogen contained in the water.

An NFT technique was also proposed where the affluent from the fish tank is drawn off to hydroponic sand/gravel beds. But this method soon lost favor when the affluent lines became too easily clogged by sediments dropped by the fish. What now seems to be in favor and what may be a hydroponic technique for the future is something designed along the following lines:

1. A fish tank provided with an agitator to increase oxygen and keep sediment in solution.
2. A rotating biofilter to mineralize ammonia to nitrate and nitrite.
3. A settling tank to remove solids suspended in the affluent.
4. A gravel filled hydroponic tank in which to grow the desired plants.
5. An equalizing water reservoir with a relift pump to keep the water at certain levels in the fish tank.
6. Emergency oxygen tanks between the reservoir and the fish tanks.

This is an indoor-outdoor plan. Everything is kept inside at indoor temperatures. Only the hydroponic tanks and the settling tank are kept outside. Because of the temperature control fish grow faster in this system than in the average farm growing pond. But tomatoes, though surpassing the production of the same fruit in soil, only climb to 60-70% of normal hydroponic output.

Oyster shell is used to protect against acidification of the system. This also protects against nitrate buildup. Plants actively remove phosphorus and nitrogen from the affluent and this helps the fish to grow better. Deficiencies of trace elements are offset with the addition of magnesium and chelated iron.

Sand And gravel techniques: Two different systems instead of one:

Sand and gravel are still used with success throughout the world and in some areas of the United States. Some operations use only sand, others use only gravel, and there are those who use a combination of both as suggested in Section One. The sand technique is particularly suited to arid regions.

Superior Farming in Tucson, AZ has over 11 acres devoted to sand culture. Sun Valley Hydroponics in Fabens, TX has 10 acres of sand culture. Quechan Environmental Farms on the Fort Yuma Indian Reservation in California has 5 acres. Many Middle East countries now have sand operations.

SAND: Use river-wash sand which drains easily and doesn't puddle. The greenhouse floor must be packed down before laying plastic sheets which should overlap 3-5 feet. Drain pipes are placed on top of the plastic at intervals of 4-6 feet, depending upon the fineness and draining characteristics of the sand. Drain pipes can be up to 2 inches in diameter, with cuts 1/3 of the way through the pipe. The pipes are placed with the cuts facing down. One end of the pipe must be above ground or sand level so it can be cleaned out with a roto-rooter.

Since waste drainage is not recycled, drip irrigation is used with sand beds. A spaghetti piping (furnished by such people as Chapin) supplies nutrient to each plant. For adequate drainage the bed slope should be 3-4 inches per hundred feet. Irrigation systems of this sort deliver 10 gallons per minute for 5000 sq ft. The system should be set up where no more than 10% nutrient is wasted. Tensiometers and flow valves are necessary to make the operation work well on a consistent basis. Main line water pressure should be at 20-40 pounds per sq inch. Flow valves will reduce the pressure to the 3 pound pressure needed for the drip lines.

Leaching of the beds is necessary when bed salt levels reach 2000 ppm. A time clock will monitor waterings which can be as many as 6 a day, depending upon the crop and the climate. The nutrient solution in the tank doesn't have to be changed (this is an open system), but the pH should be checked daily. Of course this also depends upon your water supply and its pH.

The advantages of sand over gravel are: open system, lower construction costs, better water retention, easier to manage, drain pipes don't plug as easily because sand lets the roots grow laterally, sand is readily available. The disadvantages are: steam or chemical fumigation must be used after each crop, salt accumulates more quickly but regular leaching with clean water can keep this down, drip lines become clogged now and then.

GRAVEL:

Most gravel systems use sub-irrigation. Submerged pipe is used to flood the beds to an inch or two from the surface (a good way to get rid of nematodes). After the nutrient is allowed to stand for awhile, it is drained back to the reservoir. This is a closed system - the nutrient is used over and over again. Depending upon the crop the nutrient is changed completely every few weeks. Flooding times are dictated by the size of the crop, type of gravel and weather conditions. Gravel media will be irrigated almost twice as often as sand. Large pipes are used because the flooding and draining must be accomplished within thirty minutes. All of the solution must be drained. And the temperature of the nutrient should not be allowed to fall below average night-time temperatures.

Various methods are used to flood the beds. Plenums and flumes (for outdoors) are used to let the water drain from the beds. Sluice gates and sumps are also used. Beds set in terrace fashion can be manually controlled - make certain the first bed is full before allowing it to drain to the next bed below. The trickle system uses gravel the diameter of 1/8 to 1/4 inch. This has some advantages over sub-irrigation. These advantages are: not as much root clogging, better aeration, simpler design and operation, lower cost. The disadvantages are: lines can get pulled out by careless workers, nutrient goes straight down from the plant rather than fanning out laterally.

Gravel culture has many benefits but one of the best is its economical use of nutrient. Since the same nutrient can be used again and again (within certain limits), costs can be kept lower. The pH is easier to maintain in gravel cultures. Gravel is good for giving plenty of fresh air to plant roots, and gravel is easier to automate and sterilize. But gravel does have temperature extremes from hot to cold and it doesn't give firm anchorage to larger plants. Smooth-type gravel needs irrigation more than rough-types.

Further items of interest:

- Formaldehyde sterilization for sand/gravel beds: 1 part Formaline to 100 parts water. Fill beds to above surface. Let stand overnight. Drain completely and rinse 3 times with water. Cover beds with plastic to keep in the fumes overnight. Humans use gas masks.

- Do you have doubts about chlorinated water and how it will effect your crops? Have no fear. As long as the chlorine content is no more than 1 ppm you'll have no problems. Even higher concentrations of up to 10 ppm most likely won't hurt the plants' commercial viability.

- Use nutrient solution to irrigate salts away in a one-way medium such as agricultural rockwool. Otherwise if you use clear water only you'll find the increased E.C. will draw out moisture from the plants and cause them to wilt. In this case over-irrigation of nutrient solution by 10% is advisable. Also remember that plants, like humans, don't like wide temperature swings. This applies to the nutrient solution too.

- Superabsorbents seem to be the coming thing. These are tiny particles which when mixed with media and soaked with water/nutrient will retain that water/nutrient much longer than in a normal media situation. Superabsorbents provide water/nutrient to plants only when the root absorbs the fluid and when the plant presses against them. Superabsorbents can also be mixed with media other than peat. In case of intermittent peat shortages, this bark mixture can replace peat moss and vermiculite.

- Did you know that red mulch (even painted red sheets) can cause tomatoes to produce 20% higher yields than if you use a black mulch? Clemson University scientists have a patent on the idea. It's a technique which uses phytochrome, a protein which is color sensitive.

- A problem which many of us could do without has recently attracted attention. You now have to be aware of the interactions between your media and your fertilizer. There's a lot of micro-organic activity in even the cleanest media. These organisms are very important as to how much nitrogen is absorbed by the plant's system. Nitrogen deficiency can occur when these organisms deplete the available nitrogen. Admittedly there are much less of these organisms in peat than in soil. But even in peat they do enough damage to allow ammonium to accumulate and thus present a hazard to the plant. Cure: don't use ammonium based nitrogen. And use fresh peat right away.

- Alkalinity, not acid, is the determining factor in nutrient availability within a growing medium. Since water is constantly changing, the smart grower would do well to have his water supply tested at least twice a year by a reputable laboratory. Preferably more often than that. Some growers have bought greenhouses without previously checking the water supply. Others have built greenhouses on raw land and then drilled a well to find out the water is unsatisfactory. Most water problems are buffered in soil but in a hydroponic medium there are few buffers. A good water analysis not only checks for alkalinity but also concentrations of nitrogen, sodium,, magnesium, aluminum, copper, iron, the fluorides, the chlorides and soluble salts. All except soluble salts are expressed in ppm and can be checked against Peters/Terra-lite lab water analysis guidelines.

CHAPTER 10

RECIPES FOR GROWING VARIOUS CROPS

Tomatoes: General growing procedures:

Everybody wants to grow them, and we continually warn people to be careful. But if they must get involved to do so on a limited basis. Greenhouse tomato growing is a difficult business - because of the competition not only locally but also from other states and other countries. In most cases tomatoes are nowhere near as income productive as other crops, such as foliage and potted plants (and flowers). Competition with field grown tomatoes can be terrific. This information is provided for those who just have to raise tomatoes or who have a unique marketing situation where tomatoes are quite viable for profit. First of all when marketing tomatoes, divide them into three groups. Premium grade which you will sell to your best customers and who demand the best, good grade which you can sell to fast-food outlets and at your own roadside stand, and culls which you can keep for your own table.

Your best profits will result when you use the best transplants/seed in order to get more production. **DON'T CUT CORNERS HERE - BUY THE BEST!** Some varieties you should consider are Michigan-Ohio hybrid, Florabel, Tropic, and Caruso. A greenhouse tomato should be globular and smooth, have deep red skin and flesh, be 3-4 inches in diameter and set fruit well under a wide range of temperature and light conditions. Use treated seed only. Choose those varieties which are resistant to fusarium wilt, mosaic virus, nematodes and verticillium wilt. These should be listed on the seed package as F,M,N,V in any order. Germinate your own seed as indicated in Section One, except with tomatoes use Jiffy cubes (at most suppliers) or rockwool cubes (for NFT operations).

We recommend you use the bag technique for tomatoes. You won't constantly have to monitor the nutrient solution because it will never get out of balance like a closed re-circulating system does. The mixture inside the bag should be between soggy like a sponge (but not dripping wet) and dry. Check the bottom of the bags for moisture; if moisture is coming out at the bottom then the media is too wet. Tomato stalks should be tied to strong overhead wires (10-12 gauge) which also should be supported every four feet. Tomato vines should have all suckers removed as they appear. There should be only one main stem. The rule of thumb for removing the lower leaves: after a hand of fruit (where the blossoms occur) has set, remove the leaves below the hand of fruit when that fruit becomes as large as quarters. This applies to all varieties except the cherry tomato. As the vine grows, carefully lower the bare stem but not more than one or two feet at a time. Do this during the daytime when there is more heat in the greenhouse - otherwise you might break the vine or stem. Re-tie the top end at the overhead wire. This procedure should only be done after the vine has reached the top of the wire. If you are growing tomatoes continually year-round, start your new seedlings and pinch off the top end of the growing vine 4-5 weeks before the time you have set for termination of the crop.

Set tomato bag containers (or in any other media such as beds) at 18 inch intervals and on a diagonal coursing. The diagonal distance and horizontal distance will always be 18 inches. You will cut your production if you set too close or too far apart. Tomatoes do best at temperatures between 60 degrees F at night and 88 degrees F during the day. The humidity for good pollination should be around 60-70%

Opinions vary but most growers believe the best tasting tomatoes are grown in peat mixtures in polyethylene bags. Those grown in rockwool don't taste as good and don't have as good a color. Here is a recipe or one kind of peat mix. This so-called New Jersey mix makes one cubic yard: 9 bushels sphagnum peat moss; 10 lbs 10-10-10 fertilizer; 9 bushels vermiculite; 3 lbs magnesium sulphate; 10 lbs agricultural limestone; 5 lbs calcium sulphate. This is for long-term use. The added nutrients get the plant off to a fast start. You still feed your regular nutrient mix at stated times.

Other good media mixes are: 80% sand to 20% gravel, 60% gravel to 40% sawdust, 70% coarse sand to 30% sawdust, 40% perlite to 60% chopped peat moss, 50% #8 perlite (horticultural grade) to 50% vermiculite. This book recommends the perlite/peat moss mix for its lightness. You should make a fresh batch and change the mixture at the end of each crop. A crop of tomatoes could last for an entire year. Choose the mixture which is easily and inexpensively obtained. Use white plastic on the floor and around the bags to give extra warmth and light in the winter (see bag technique in last part of Section One). Tests prove that tomatoes whose roots are warmed will produce anywhere from 25% to 75% more fruit. Root-zone warming can come in handy here.

If you're using gravel beds or mixes, keep an eye on them. They dry out in a few hours. Also, in order to pollinate efficiently, you need to shake or vibrate the vine every day. The number one disease for tomatoes is bacterial leaf spot. To control this disease stop overhead watering. And keep the area close to the greenhouse mown and free of weeds.

SPECIFIC ATTENTION TO NUTRIENT BALANCE WILL MAKE THE DIFFERENCE IN YOUR GROWING ATTEMPTS AND WILL BE THE No. 1 KEY TO PROFIT. For optimum growth, you must keep all 16 elements in balance. These 16 elements are:

MAJOR ELEMENTS: calcium, carbon, hydrogen, magnesium, nitrogen, oxygen, phosphorus, potassium, sulphur.
MICRO ELEMENTS: chlorine, copper, iron, manganese, molybdenum, zinc, boron. Carbon, hydrogen and oxygen are furnished by carbon monoxide in the air and in water. You must furnish the rest.

Why not use the commercial mixes, for simplicity's sake? Such as Peters or Chem-Gro 10-8-22. And be sure to follow the instructions. Some commercial mixes will need additives, such as Epsom salts which gives trace elements and boron. Some will not need anything extra.

Check and be sure before using. You still want to mix your own fertilizer? Try Hoagland's formula.

Use at 1/2 strength when plant growth starts and until first fruit; then use at full strength until the end of the crop.

MACRO nutrient solution:

Ammonium Phosphate (mono) . . . . . . 4 milliliters per gallon
Potassium nitrate . . . . 23 ml/gal
Calcium nitrate w/4 parts water   . . . . . 15 ml/gal (20 for fruiting)
Magnesium sulphate w/7 parts water   . . 8 ml/gal

MICRO nutrient solution:

Boric acid . . . . 11 grams per gallon
Manganese chloride w/4 parts water . . . 7 g/gal
Zinc sulphate w/7 parts water . . . . 1 g/gal
Copper sulphate w/5 parts water . . . . . 1/3 g/gal
Molybdic acid w/1 part water . . . . 1/10 g/gal

Add micronutrient solution (which has been mixed separately) to the macrosolution at the rate of 4 milliliters to each gallon of macronutrient solution. After the micronutrient has been added to the macronutrient add the following: 4 ml of 0.5% iron chelate to each gallon of total solution. The only measuring devices you will need are those for milliliter, gram and gallon. These can be purchased locally. To make batches larger than one gallon, multiply all of the above by 50, 100, 1000. Do not go above 1000 as some of the elements will precipitate at higher volumes and will not be available for plant use. Other tomato facts: E.C. of the salts in the nutrient solution should be 2.5 at planting time. Some growers feel you should increase this to 5.0 when the plant has reached its true fourth leaf. When flowering starts you should reduce to 3.0. And reduce again to 2.5 when harvest starts and until crop's end. Other growers feel that 2.5 is all right from start to finish - for both tomatoes and cucumbers. Experimentation will help you decide which reading is best for you.

Avoid these damages when preparing tomatoes for market: bruising, puncturing, packing too tightly, and rough handling during transit. The best storing temperature is 55 degrees F.

CROP INTERFACING is just fine for tomatoes. You can earn more dollars while you're waiting on the tomato crop. Plant bibb or leaf lettuce between the tomato plants while the tomato plants are still young and haven't grown tall. You could also have hanging baskets of ornamental tomatoes. What about summer months when tomatoes are coming in from the field? Why not run a crop of oriental vegetables through this season? Or some bedding plants, foliage plants or other seasonal crops? You could also do some custom growing for specialty floral shops.

Tomato production takes up about 60% of your space. It takes 120 days to get the first fruit. There should be plenty of room for extra profits.

Lettuce: General growing and selling tips:

Growing lettuce hydroponically is a demanding job. Hydroponics is not a short cut to success. As in any business the only short cut to success is knowledge of your product, its market, and a desire to pay attention to detail. However the real reason for failure in lettuce cropping is inattention to cost management and marketing. Growing isn't the real problem; selling the crop for a profit is. For some growers, growing lettuce has become a year-round business. Their ability to stay in business depends upon customer loyalty in the winter and then matching prices with field-grown tomatoes in the summer. The problem? Perhaps these growers haven't sold nutrition strongly enough to their buying public. They have poor customer identity.

Once you get past the two-person or family operation, labor, high energy costs and high-cost structures will eat up your time and profit. If you settle your goals on the small finely tuned market, an efficient housing and growing situation, you won't have interference from the large competitors. The large grower cannot profitably handle small, individualized markets.

Fresh hydroponic lettuce demands higher prices than the field-grown. And in some cases hydroponic lettuce can be harvested more quickly: in summer, within 4-6 weeks; in winter, within 10-12 weeks. The Japanese use extra lighting and make it happen faster. See lighting in next chapter because the extra cost of lighting might come in handy during the winter when, if you can get a crop to market sooner, you can gain more profit. Some suggested lettuce varieties are: Bibb, Red Leaf or Oak Leaf, Ostinata, Black Seeded Simpson, Columbus, Vasco, Pinto, Marbello. Head lettuce isn't profitable - not yet. It takes too long to form a suitable head. Lettuce can be grown in gravel beds or on horticultural rockwool slabs (about 30 inches by 12 inches by 3 inches). But the following NFT methods have been used with great success throughout the world.

THE NUTRIENT TABLE: This is a long wide table (usually as long as the greenhouse) which is 4-6 inches deep and sealed with a sheet of plastic that is replaced at the end of the crop. Large rigid one inch slabs of styrofoam are floated upon the nutrient solution which is constantly pumped from one end of the table to the other where it is picked up and recirculated. The styrofoam floats like a boat on a sea of nutrient. The same pump can be used to aerate the liquid. Lettuce seedlings grown in 2 inch rockwool cubes are then anchored in holes drilled 6 inches apart diagonally and horizontally on the board.

The styrofoam slabs must fit together to keep out light and prevent the growth of algae. **THIS KEEPING THE ROOTS IN THE DARK IS ESSENTIAL IN NFT.** The holes in the styrofoam are so tapered that the plugs won't fall through when positioned for growth. The advantages of this system are: you plant at one end of the greenhouse and you harvest at the other, a clean operation will keep out disease, when you do get a disease in the system (which doesn't happen that often) you can inject the proper remedy into the nutrient to solve the problem. The disadvantages are: you have to regularly monitor the solution to make certain all elements are kept in their initial balance, the long tables require substantial support.

NFT TROUGHS (with light caps): This method is a modified form of the NFT table described above. But here you use high impact PVC with ultra-violet inhibitors. The pipes are spaced perpendicular to the sides of the greenhouse and 6 inches apart. These pipes all parallel each other and empty into a center collecting pipe which runs down the center of the greenhouse. The incline of these pipes is 1:100 (1 ft in 100 ft or 6 inches in 50 ft). This is to make certain the last few plants at the end of the trough get proper nutrition. The nutrient is allowed to flow through the pipes at about 1/2 inch in depth. The seedlings (usually in rockwool or peat moss cubes) are placed in pre-drilled holes in the PVC pipes which can be moved separately to any distance apart you wish. At the start they are next to each other; as the crop grows they are spaced further apart. Sometimes they are so set up that a crop can be planted at one end and be harvested at the other end of the greenhouse. Matting is sometimes used inside the pipes to give capillary feeding to plant roots. The advantages and disadvantages are the same as for the NFT table except you usually don't have to aerate the system. Some kind of swab must be used for cleaning out the pipes at the end of a crop.

NFT troughs with retrievable belts: This system is the same as the above but with the following exception. Light-excluding belts are used as caps on the troughs. The crop has been planted in this top belt which can be pulled off the trough and retrieved at the other end of the house. The crop is harvested as the belt is pulled in. A new crop can be planted at the same time on a new belt. Short belts can be handled manually. Longer belts are more high-tech.

The nutrient solution should have an electrical conductivity (E.C.) of 1.8. Use a commercially prepared mixture. If you mix your own, you can use the Hoagland formula given for tomatoes and add 75% more calcium nitrate. Another tip: before using agricultural rockwool saturate it with water before planting the seed or seedling. Want to grow Bibb lettuce in the summer? During 100 degree days? Place a water chiller (a refrigeration unit) in the nutrient solution inside the nutrient tank and keep the temperature of the nutrient solution at about 75 degrees F. A one horsepower unit large enough to chill a thousand gallon tank costs around $2,000. This trick is used by a large grower in Florida.

NFT A-frames:

Same principal as the above techniques except the A- frame uses pipes or gutters on both sides of the frame. Six to ten parallel gutters run from top to bottom. Most growers aerate the nutrient at the tap (or top). Must have a North-South orientation to get adequate lighting. An incline of 1:30 is used to promote faster movement of the nutrient. For high density production the Irish use the A-frame or arch system. This is especially true for **strawberries**. The A-frame is designed with piping staggered like an incline railway on both sides of the arch. Using NFT techniques the Irish growers feed the plants which are anchored in the piping. When the nutrient reaches the bottom, it is pumped back to the top and run down again. Older NFT methods of laying metal or PVC "gullies" on the greenhouse floor were too stringent for the Irish. The greenhouse floor has to be too evenly "shaved" to get the proper flow from one end to the other. So the Irish use the M.J. Maher system of planting tomatoes in double rows. These rows are laid out on matting or rockwool strips. Drip irrigation is used, and since the plantings slope toward the center drain, no excess flooding occurs. The slope of the matting doesn't matter nor does the solution depth which runs off the the center drain.

This system gives the benefits of NFT without the high initial costs. Root zone warming is also used - to great advantage both in plant growth and in fuel savings. If the roots are kept warm, the air around the plant can be kept at a cooler temperature. Maher also suggested not having low nutrient flow rates because not enough oxygen is absorbed at the lower flow rates. The Irish have determined there is no difference in the quality of fruits or plants from those grown in soil or those grown hydroponically. The only difference is the increased production by using hydroponics.

Lettuce on the "Archway": It has been calculated that by using the archway concept as much as $160,000 can be grossed on 1/3 acre - if you sell at 50 cents per head (leaf or Bibb). How? Because Irish growers can get 8 - 9 crops per year! The arch or A-frame concept gives you more than double the growing space. You can get 34 plants per square yard! **HOW DO THEY DO IT?** First the archway is sited in a N-S direction. Second, PVC troughs 4 inches wide and 3 inches deep are lanted in a slope of 1 inch to every 30 feet and are thus staggered from the top of the arch to the bottom. Matting is placed in the bottom of the troughs and drip irrigation is used for feeding. (Here drip irrigation means allowing the nutrient to flow slowly from top to bottom.) The lettuce seeds are planted in two-inch rockwool cubes. When the seeds have sprouted and grown to seedling size, the plants are placed in the PVC tubing at intervals 8 inches apart.

One grower has his troughs staggered twelve feet high! But the best pattern seems to be six double rows on each side of the arch or "A". The Irish also use 1 1/4 inch diameter PBV pipe in 6 1/2 ft lengths. They drill 3/4 inch holes every 7 5/8 inches. Then they insert the seedling's roots into the hole and allow the leaves to rest on top of the tube. The results are very good. The grower can market "clean" lettuce because nothing has ever touched the plant except the nutrient flow at the roots. In our opinion, this size tubing is too small. It promotes root clogging and poor plant growth at the far end of the tube. But the Irish say they have no problem with it. There have been no root death or other diseases for these year-round operations.

Marketing tip: Package the lettuce in separate open plastic bags, pack in cartons and number according to size of carton and customer order. **LETTUCE STORES VERY POORLY - HAVE A READY MARKET FOR IT!** Even refrigeration doesn't help much. Just imagine how your freshly picked lettuce will taste when compared to that brought by refrigerated trucks from 1,000 to 2,000 miles away! Some of those growers have to keep lettuce cool for as long as a week! What can they do? If they don't have a ready market, they must refrigerate. Here is where you save money and make your operation more successful: set up your marketing so well that you won't have to refrigerate. **IT CAN BE DONE AND IS BEING**

DONE! Lettuce can also be harvested cube, root and all. This usually convinces the customer that you are running a clean operation.

Cucumbers: Nutrition and care:

Cucumbers are one of the three top hydroponic vegetable crops. Only European varieties are used because they are burpless, seedless and thin-skinned. They must be grown inside a greenhouse and under controlled conditions. Some varieties available are: Sandra, Tosca 70, Corona, Straight Eight, Farbio, Farona, Profito, Brucona, Brunex, Vitalis, Salvador, Brudania, DaLeva, LaReine, Rocket, Brilliant, Uniflora D, and Pandex. Choose according to your area's climate. European cucumbers are self-pollinating and will not reproduce from seed. Most blossoms are female. You should remove all male flowers, if any. Do not allow bees inside the greenhouse as they will cause the plants to produce poor quality fruit. Poor quality fruit also results from low light, low air temperature, low humidity, and low carbon dioxide. European cucumbers when harvested should be wrapped in saran wrap because their thin skin cannot retain inner moisture. They can be eaten without being peeled.

Fertilization: Use a commercial formula designed for this crop or use the basic Hoagland formula given in the tomato discussion. Most growers use 1/2 of the original formula until the first fruit is set. Then they go to full strength. This applies only to macronutrients; the micronutrients always stay the same. Some successful growers suggest you add more nitrogen when the plant is 4-5 feet tall. A good source of extra nitrogen would be calcium nitrate. Use 1 teaspoon per gallon of water and use a quart of this mixture 2 times a week per plant. You can also use 1 teaspoon of dry calcium nitrate per plant by strewing it once a week on the surface of the media which surrounds the plant.

Watering: Normally this is done every 1 1/2 to 2 hours for mature plants - 15 minutes at a time. This will depend upon the metering system being used. One way to determine water needs is to check the overhead leaves. If the top leaves start to wilt, you'll need to increase your watering times. But don't use more than necessary. You want to reduce vegetative growth in order to have better fruit set and development. After fruit set, water should be slowly increased. The medium shouldn't get too wet as this will attract fungus gnats and their larvae will eat the roots of the seedlings.

Other conditions: E.C. should not go above 2.5 millimhos/cm. Also the fertilizer must be watched when you restrict the water flow. The pH level should be between 6.5 and 6.8. If it's too high, you can lower by adding white vinegar (in a small operation). If it's too low, add baking soda. Larger operations will use volume acidifiers. The growing temperature is 70-90 degrees with relative humidity at 70%. The entire greenhouse must be used for cucumbers only. This gives a more efficient operation.

Culture: Plant seeds lying flat - one per planting block, if you're using rockwool or peat cubes. Transplant the cubes after seed germination to their permanent growing medium. Since proper pruning is necessary to keep the plant from putting on too much fruit, you'll want to reduce the abortion rate by doing the following:

A. Prune all growth, including fruit and side shoots, up to 2 ft above the medium. Some growers prune all fruit as high as the tenth leaf node. This lets the root system gain vigorous growth. Plant clips are used under the leaf stem at every 2 ft. Attach the clip to the support wire or cord.

B Harvest fruit at 12-16 inches in length.

C. Don't let more than one fruit form at a leaf axis.

D. When a lateral grows from a leaf axis, allow only one fruit and two leaves to form. Then pinch off the terminal end of the lateral and pinch off all other laterals which may form. Do this with every leaf axis.

E. After a fruit is harvested, pinch off the lateral at the main stem.

F. When the stem reaches the top of your support, allow two laterals to form and pinch off the main stem. As the two laterals grow downward in an umbrella effect, treat each of them as you did the main stem and follow through with all of the above. Allow these two new stems to grow about 2/3 of the way downward.

The umbrella system gives some growers a crop which lasts 10 months and which produces as much as 100 European cucumbers per plant.

The bag system: Plant one plant every other bag. When this crop terminates, plant in the bags you haven't used. This method will yield six short crops per year. You sterilize and re-plant the used bags after termination of the second crop. And repeat the process. Of course, you grow only to the top wire and then start over again. Five-gallon pots can be used instead of bags; these won't have to be replaced at the end of the season. The bag system is especially adaptable to the V-shaped trellis effect. To achieve this effect, row widths should be five feet apart. In-line distance between bags would be 14-16 inches. Tie to overhead wires which are 2 1/2-3 ft apart. Tie each plant alternately to each side - giving a V-shaped effect as you look down the row. This method will give more light to each plant.

At crop termination: a few days before you decide to do this, pull the roots of the plants from the medium. Shake the roots clean. Shut off water and nutrient. In a few days, the plants will have dehydrated, be much lighter in weight and easier to dispose of. Take the plants outside at a distance and either bury or burn them. Then go through the entire greenhouse and clean everything in sight. Sterilize all growing bags or pots and all nutrient tanks. **DO THIS ALWAYS BEFORE STARTING A NEW CROP.** This applies to all crops, not just cucumbers.

Some northern growers have increased cucumber harvests by as much as 40% by using carbon dioxide enrichment up to 1000-1500 ppm. Cucumbers are moderately salt tolerant. But only for the young plants. Saline solutions up to 3000 ppm reduce yields by as much as 25%.

Foliage: Specific plants = specific needs.

Most foliage plants are descendants from natives of the tropics where bright sunshine and abundant shade abound. All amid copious rains. You must always keep in mind that these plants have begun in surroundings where the forest floor holds very little soil. The forest floor of the tropics is mostly a fine webbing of roots and leaves. When it rains, the water falls on the forest floor and rapidly disappears. There is nothing to hold the water. It simply flows away as fast as it falls. Keeping this in mind, you will understand why you cannot place one of these plants, say dieffenbachia, ficus or dracaena, in the usual pot medium and keep watering it over and over. You will drown it. This type of plant likes to catch its moisture "on the run". You must wait until the root ball is almost dry and then you give the plant a thorough soaking. Most of these kinds of plants do not like bright sunlight.

Most foliage sold in the United States is grown in Florida or California. Growers in other parts of the country will buy seedlings or started crops and finish them off for their local markets. This cuts down on the transportation costs of the completed plant and affords the local grower the opportunity to compete with the growers in Florida and California.

Water: the pH should be 5.5 70 6.5. Iron, though essential, if over-supplied, can cause plants to grow in an ungainly manner. Fluoride and chlorine should be kept at a minimum, the first at zero, the second at no more than 50 ppm. If you are on the city water main, you can get this information from the water department. Again, water thoroughly and give a long rest in between. **THIS IS THE BIGGEST CAUSE FOR LOSSES IN THE INDUSTRY:** not paying attention to the plant's specific water needs. Another cause for loss: not paying attention to the difference in temperature around the root system and in the atmosphere outside the pot.

Frequent watering gives large luxurious plants. But in order to sell them and get them to do well in the customer's home, you have to slowly reduce the frequency and amount of your water. This will allow the root systems to grow larger. You should also reduce fertilization during this period. You also have to watch for soluble salt in your water: too much will prompt you to reduce or eliminate fertilizer - particularly at the end of the crop period.

Since plant canopies deflect water away from the pots, overhead watering is not recommended. The resultant moisture remaining on the leaves will make the plants susceptible to disease. Hand watering or drip irrigation from tubing are better. But the workers performing this chore must be taught how to do it. Most workers will not understand highly developed systems. You have to choose a simple method and tell them how you want it done. Tubing, even when regulated by sensors, must be checked form time to time for clogging, etc. Another watering system is the capillary method. Here the pots are set on a capillary matting and water is drawn up from the matting and into the pot. Some growers use beds of gravel to achieve the same effect. They keep the water level in the gravel beds at specific levels for specific lengths of time.

Fertilizer: Fertilizer has to be adjusted to the amount of available light and the plant's needs. If you don't balance fertilizer intake with light intensity, you will have a poor crop. Cloudy weather or a shaded greenhouse will cause the plants to use less fertilizer. Some growers make the mistake of using shading to induce dark green growth whereas fertilizer and more light would be the better answer. If you have a fluoride problem and cannot get rid of it, keep the pH above 6.0. Temperature is another fertilizer control - the higher the temperature, the more fertilizer the plant will use. Most foliage plants won't do well below 65 degrees F. From 55-60 degrees F (and lower) most foliage plants will not use iron which is necessary to make them green.

Slow-release fertilizers are used the most. Instead of mixing your own, it is better to buy an industry brand which you can get from your supplier. Fertilizer is often mixed with the medium before planting. If you apply dry fertilizer, you must do it evenly to prevent localized root burn. Since this has to be done by hand (if you do it overhead it will get down inside the plant leaves and burn), it can become time-consuming and expensive. That's why most commercial growers use liquid fertilization with irrigation tubing. But a two- person operation needn't worry about this at the outset.

Foliar fertilization: This has become popular lately because you can use the same apparatus to spray insecticide and herbicide. Generally speaking, fertilization rates depend upon: the plant, the amount of light, the temperature, the plant's natural growth rate and the size of the pot. Large plants in small pots require more fertilizer than usual. For small pots (1-4 inches in diameter): fertilize weekly or every other week unless you are using liquid or slow-release fertilizer. For larger pots: fertilize weekly to monthly unless on liquid or slow-release. A liquid program would be one which is diluted to suit the plant and which would be constantly fed. The most desirable general fertilizer for foliage plants should be in the following ratios: 3-1-2, that is nitrogen = 3, phosphate = 1, and potash = 2. You can also avoid high salt problems in your local water supply by not letting the medium dry out by more than 50%.

Media: It must be light, porous. It must allow for quick drainage as well as have plenty of space for good air circulation. Why? Again, you are duplicating the "jungle" climate from which these plants originally came. Small growers should order prepared potting mixes from their supplier. The mix should suit the plant.

Fern: This plant can put you in the green in a big way!

Ferns are coming back. Once quite the rage in Victorian England, you can now see them almost everywhere. Victorians even obliged Captain Bligh of the famous "Mutiny on the Bounty" to bring back loads of fern from the tropics. Which should tell you something else: most fern were originally native to the tropics. That's why most fern like high humidity, filtered sunlight and low-strength nutrition.

Select your varieties with care: Some popular varieties when young do not have a good appearance. Others when young look good but become stringy when mature. The difference may be seen between 2-3 inch pots and 4-6 inch pots. Since the customer is the boss, sell the small good-looking plants for terrariums and similar diminutive displays. The best thing to do with the others is to grow them to maturity and reap the higher profits. Consider also the following:

propagating stock available at all times, propagation must be true from spore, bud propagation must be able to occur in sufficient amounts, meristem propagation must not risk the death of the parent plant, spore must stay viable for some time and easily germinate in a variety of media. You must select fern which are resistant to the following: nematodes, Botrytis and some fungus attacks.

Popular varieties which are being offered today are: Victoria Brake, Common Maidenhair, Boston Fern, Sword Fern, Staghorn Fern and Bird's Nest Fern. Here are just a few varieties of just one category, the Boston Fern: *Fluffy Ruffle, Trevillian, *Rooseveltii Plumosa *Splendida, Whitman, *Norwood, Irish Lace, Wagner. The asterisk indicates the most popular varieties. Fertilize these fern with a half-strength mixture, usually one heavy in nitrogen. Peters provides a good formula for fern. The medium must always be moist to the touch - but not swampy or wet. As usual, constant dilute feeding does the trick.

Propagation: For branching rhizome fern (the rhizome is part of the root structure), cut off the branching part only and leave the growing tip to the parent. For non-branching rhizome fern, look for a bud swelling. Cut halfway beyond the swelling and halfway through the rhizome. A couple of months later, a side shoot will come from the bud. Complete the original cut and transplant. Wash clean the cut ends of the rhizome and dust with a fungicide before planting. The fungicide should be at half-strength. Cut off half of the leaf front to give better root growth. Plant bare-rooted fern roots in a fan-like spread over a cone-shaped mound of medium and cover with more of the medium.

Spore propagation: Shake the ripened fronds over a sheet of paper and tap the paper to get rid of the chaff. Transplant the spore in a glass bowl or other suitable container which has about 1/2 inch of gravel and about 2 inches of vermiculite on top of the gravel. Moisten with distilled water, cover with a plastic film, and place in a bright spot but not in direct sunlight. When the spore become seedlings, spoon out in little clumps and plant in 3 inch pots. Separate the individual fern when more growth has been attained. The pH range for fern lies between 5.0 and 7.5. In the list given above, all of them like a pH of 6.5 to 7.0. The Common Maidenhair likes 5.5 to 6.5. If the above procedures seem a little too much for you consider buying fern already at the 3 inch stage and then grow them to market size. Be sure to find a supplier on whom you can depend. Also consider, as most growers don't, introducing new and interesting varieties to the market. Here you will have to start from scratch. You will also need extra space because it takes 5-9 months to get from spore to plants in the 3 inch stage.

Some specifics: Victoria Brake like humidity; propagate from rhizome or spore. Common Maidenhair is propagated from spore at the end of the large veins. Boston Fern sometimes reverts to the wild stage from spore; so propagate from detached runner buds. Water large plants by immersing the entire pot in water and then drain. Sword Fern is propagated from runners or spore. Staghorn Fern is propagated from spore near the "antlers". Use a mixture of fibrous material and webbing for a hold-to-the-wall kind of plaque. Then place the Staghorn Fern on a backing of cork bark and keep humid. Bird's Nest Fern is propagated from spore. High humidity is required.

The public wants showy ferns which are compact and not stringy. The fronds should be close together and the plant must be symmetric overall. In some cases, for indoor use customers like small or medium type plants. Most customers want ferns which can stand low humidity, little light and able to adapt to sporadic watering. Obviously this attitude promotes more business for you! The fern won't last under those conditions. A good marketing technique: furnish information on the care of the plant which the customer buys. This could be imprinted on the tag which comes with the plant. **(AS YOU KNOW, THIS SHOULD BE DONE WITH ALL PLANTS, NOT JUST FERN!)** Other markets for large showy fern are interior decorators and landscape designers, providing in the latter case that the fern are hardy.

Herbs: They can add sizzle to your profits!

Herbs can be grown a lot faster with hydroponics. However the main criticism against hydroponic herbs is that they lack pep or taste. So get your ducks in a row. Get your production methods down pat in order to insure that your herbs do in fact have plenty of pep and taste. Don't commit yourself to growing herbs hydroponically until you're sure these herbs will be just as good smelling and tasting as those grown in soil. You'll have to experiment a little. If you stay aware of each herb's fertilizer and culture requirements you should be able to keep your problems to a minimum.

The herbal market is growing rapidly because chefs are discovering they can get fresh herbs grown close at home. If you can furnish clean fresh herbs in small units of supply but with some variety, the customer is yours. You don't want to go broke trying to grow too many varieties. Basically the following herbs can be profitably grown: water cress, basil, mint, rosemary, thyme, sage, tarragon and dandelion. All except dandelion can be grown in pots which will also open up the housewife market for you. A chef may only want a handful of one particular herb. But if you can satisfy all his herbal needs, you can afford to make the delivery. If you also program your deliveries within a restricted area, you can make them all that much more profitable. Your profit per square foot can be as high as $50-$60!

The profit lies not only in furnishing fresh edible herbs to restaurants and markets but also in marketing dried herbs, fragrant herbal oils and for ornamental uses in landscaping. Suppose you over-produce one herb? A very high profit idea to exploit would be a product line which utilizes this over-supply. You could market herbal butters, herbal jellies, dried sachets. And you might find this end of the market more exciting than the fresh herb end.

The herbal market appears to be a growing one for at least several more years. The locally grown herb is attracting more and more attention. Chefs are no longer looking to Europe for such specialty items. And already one fast-food chain is featuring fresh herbs at its salad bar! Acceptance will gain momentum. Be ready to cash in on that momentum by learning and preparing yourself as much as you can.

How do you grow them? The old adage that herbs like poor soil is false. However you should not use a fertilizer which is too rich. This will give you a lot of growth but not much flavor and very little oil in the leaves. Use a fertilizer such as 5-5-5 or 10-10-10 where all three elements are in balance. Use in moderation and don't feed too often. The clue as to what's happening as far as flavor goes is this: if the growth is too lush, then quite possibly you're not getting much flavor. Most herbs grow well at temperatures between 70-80 degrees F. They like moderate fertilizer, some sun and good drainage. They do not like a soggy medium. They prefer a humidity of 40-50%. You can propagate from cuttings (3-5 inches long) taken from the new tip growth. You can also propagate by layering. Most growers grow directly from seed which is less labor intensive. The only advantage of using propagation methods other than seed is that you have the plant sooner than you do with seeds.

Incidentals items:
- Mint prefers indirect light. Rosemary doesn't like as much water as mint and other herbs. Sage also prefers less water. French tarragon doesn't have seeds; it has to be propagated from cuttings.
- In order to make plants more compact and bushy, pinch back the growing tips of the plants. This is especially important if you are selling in individual containers for the retail market.
- Mints grow very fast underground, but present no problem if planted in pots. If mint is planted in a bed (of any kind of media) the roots will fill the entire bed. This may sound like a good idea except for one thing: when the bed gets full the quality of the plants begins to deteriorate.
- If you're growing herbs for their oils, the best time to harvest in almost all cases is when the plant begins to flower - just between bud and flower stage for most. Dandelion is a high-grade salad herb found in the poorest of homes and the finest of restaurants. Blanched or white dandelion stalks are best. These can be obtained by covering the lower parts of the stems with something which keeps out light.
- Medical houses are avidly searching for medications which can be manufactured from plants and their roots. For example, from the rosy periwinkle (Catharanthus roseus) which grows in Madagascar, scientists have obtained vinblastine which is used in the treatment of leukemia.

Water/Nutrient Runoff:

If you're not using a closed system, such as in NFT, you will need to water and use nutrient in such a way as to keep from having any run-off. This is sometimes difficult to do because good growing practices entail flushing (leaching) on a regular basis to prevent salt buildup. You may need a plastic lined pool if you find you can't limit your run-off problem. Besides it's more profitable to recirculate your water/nutruient whenever possible. You may lose up to 40% of your nutrient if you don't recirculate.

CHAPTER 11

MORE ON CROPS: Some minor varieties

Spring bulbs: How to get some welcome winter dollars: The marketing of flowering spring bulbs relies upon timing and creative decorative ability. Since bulbs cannot be rushed into blooming, this gives you an opportunity to plan your sales with precision. This also gives you time to feature creative displays with the use of baskets, indoor window boxes, small and large strawberry jars. Most important you can set up a full program of selling spring bulbs as bedding plants to landscape companies who want to give their customers "instant spring." A mass of crocus in a large basket is very appealing if you intermingle thatches of grass in among the flowers. Pots and see-through containers are quite fetching as most customers will buy the display in order to get the container.

Selling bulbs which you have already "wintered" is easier if you let the customer know that you've already done most of his work for him. All he needs to do is to plant and a few weeks later he'll have a flowering garden! With this in mind, you should start selling spring bulbs as bedding plants. Since many customers come into your outlet in spring and want spring plants, you can sell winterized bulbs by the flat! Tell the customer if he wants spring bulbs to bloom in his garden he'll have to wait until next year - unless he buys your winterized bulbs. There is a wide open market opportunity here to sell this type of "bedding plant" to landscape contractors. In Nashville, it's already being done on a small scale. The grounds of and around the state capitol are done in this way.

You can extend your selling season by having early and late blooming varieties. Remember the amount of available light dictates blooming time. So plan your sales accordingly. As usual, on each flowering plant you sell have a card attached which gives feeding and watering instructions. Remind the buyer that the bulbs should be planted outside as they will not do well in a pot after having been forced to an early bloom.

Winterizing: This is a very important procedure as these bulbs will not produce (except amaryllis, gloxinia, and calla lily) unless they've been kept at 32-45 degrees F for 8-10 weeks before being forced to bloom. For bulbs intended for landscape contractors, plant in the desired medium November 10 to 15 at 48 degrees F, drop to 41 degrees F on December 1 through 5 and keep at 32-35 degrees F until January 1 through 5. They'll be ready for landscape planting by March 16 through 28. Northern growers should do the same except they should keep the final phase at 32-35 degrees F delayed until April 1. By the way, all the bulbs while growing don't like root warming. Most growers use refrigeration to winterize - particularly if their greenhouses are occupied with other warm-natured crops. Always buy the best bulbs at the lowest prices you can find. Plan early and order early.

Narcissus: This includes tazetta or Paper Whites, Daffodils, Jonquils, Lilies of the Valley. Although some of these can be made to bloom before Christmas, most of them have better blooms later in the season. Fill your bowl or pot with any medium (usually pebbles or sand/gravel). Saturate the medium with water and drain. Plant bulb 1/2 way down into the medium. The base of the bulb should be above the water level now established in the container. Plant in groups and space one inch apart (more for larger bulbs). Keep in a ventilated, dark area at 50 degrees F for 6-8 weeks. Check the water level periodically - the roots can be in the water but not the bulb. When the shoots are 4 inches high, expose the plant to bright but not direct sunlight. **REMEMBER THAT BULBS DO NOT REQUIRE FERTILIZER. THEY FURNISH THEIR OWN FOOD.**

Plant most bulbs with their tips showing above the medium. Tulips should be treated in the same manner as narcissus. Tulips are generally wintered 6-8 weeks and planted 5-6 bulbs to the container. Grape Hyacinth are also handled in the same manner. But these should be planted 12 to a 6-inch pot and the medium kept moist at a temperature of 50-60 degrees F. They like direct sunlight.

Hyacinth, Crocus: These plants like the same medium as used with Narcissus. The medium should be kept moist while the plants are growing. If the bulbs have been planted in the fall and kept at 50 degrees F for 12 weeks, they should be at a height of 2 inches when you place them in direct light at 50 degrees F for 7-10 days. Allow 4 hours of direct sunlight daily until the buds show color. Then place them in indirect light. The temperature range for crocus is 40-65 degrees F. Do the same with Hyacinth but bring them gradually into full sunlight. Use the mammoth varieties for a showier sale!

Dwarf Iris: Treat these the same way as with Narcissus but bear in mind this plant needs good drainage. Bulb fiber or peat moss will be a better medium to use. Plant 2 inches deep - 12 to a 12-inch pot, 6 to a 6-inch pot. This plant likes a lot of light.

Amaryllis, Morea (Peacock Iris), Calla Lily, Gloxinia, Freesia: The general medium used for these plants is 1/2 peat moss mixed with 1/2 perlite and a little bone meal. For Amaryllis use a large pot 4 inches or more in diameter. Dust in with the medium mixture 1/2 teaspoon of 5-10-5 fertilizer. Plant the bulb with 1/2 sticking above the medium. Thoroughly drench the medium and let drain through holes in the bottom of the pot. Don't water again until the bulb sprouts. At that time water regularly and keep in the sun. When the plant flowers, move into indirect light. Fertilize monthly. The others have these variations: Calla lily needs its rhizomes set 3 inches deep into the medium. Gloxinia likes a humid atmosphere. All of them like 50-70 degrees F. Gloxinia also likes artificial lighting up to 16 hours a day. Freesia needs its corms set just below the surface. The Freesia medium must be kept as wet as a sponge while the plant is growing.

Cyclamen: The medium for this pant should be 2 parts peat moss, 1 part perlite mixed with a dusting of bone meal or ground agricultural limestone. Florist's or Puck are the best varieties, taking only 4-6 months to flower. The temperature range is 40-60 degrees F. They must be fed every two weeks with 5-10-5 fertilizer. Plant the tubers half in and half out of the medium. **DON'T BUY SEEDS; THEY TAKE 18 MONTHS TO FLOWER.**

SUGGESTED CROPS TO GROW: Trying something different:

Abutilon X. Hybridium: This plant is like Hibiscus but is more exotic. It flowers all year-round if brought indoors where it flowers profusely with adequate light. It's related to the Hibiscus and its blooms will last ten days! It can be an excellent plant for hanging baskets because its blooms dangle like bells. What's more important it's one of the few plants which can tolerate full sunlight. Most hanging basket choices need partial if not full shade. With spectacular blooms and foliage which looks like maple leaves, this plant offers potential for year-round sales.

Sow seeds in flat trays, cover just a little with the medium and use mist to germinate. Germination takes about three weeks at 70 degrees F. You can also use cuttings. Transplant to 4-5 inch pots with a good medium such as peat/vermiculite. Fertilizer choice should be 20-20-20.

Use a short day program for growing. Short day means 100% shade cloth coverage from 5 p.m. to 8 a.m. This will give a more compact plant. When the plants are 4-5 inches high, apply a solution of Atrinal (about 1500 ppm) as a mist and allow it to run off the leaves. There will be some leaf and stunting reaction here but this will have no effect on the final product. When the flower buds appear, apply another runoff with a solution of GA at 100 ppm. This procedure will give a plant which is well proportioned, which is compact and which displays its flowers at the best advantage. If you get ahead of schedule and need to hold over part of the crop, spray once with a solution of Cycocel at 1000 ppm.

Columbine: Why this plant? In order to gain more of the market which you may not be getting now, you should try some exotics. By exotic we mean flowers and plants which aren't the normal stock in trade of most retail outlets. There are two general kinds of Columbine: Border and Alpine. The Alpine is a smaller dwarf type; the Border rises as high as 36 inches. The best cultivars are: Silver Queen, McKana's Giant, Olympia Red-Gold, Crimson Star, Music Series, Red and Olympia Blue-White.

Propagation is best done with seed although division can also be used. Seed doesn't require as much work and is much more certain. Sow seeding sphagnum moss which is moist but not wet. The temperature should be at 60 degrees F the first 24 hours. Then refrigerate at 40 degrees F for nearly three weeks under stratification (spread out like a layer between layers of peat). After this period of time, bring them out into the light and set the temperature at 65 degrees F. After germination plant seedlings in a pre-planned potting schedule. Vernalization (when flowers are about to form after a period of cold temperature) depends upon the length of cold days and at what temperature the plants have been forced. Longer periods of cold make for quicker forcing. Sixteen to eighteen hours of light and 65 degrees F temperature will make the plants flower much faster. When placing the plants into cold storage (without light) you should pull off the older leaves to prevent diseases. The usual pot size is 4-5 inches.

The growing schedule goes something like this: about three weeks from sowing until you see the first leaf; about fifteen more weeks until vernalization where you'll get about one new leaf a week. From there it's about eight weeks for bud and flower forming, and about eight more weeks to force the bloom. To make it more economical, try the following: during the first week of July plant the seed and keep at 75 degrees F. Four weeks later transplant and keep at 65 degrees F. Three months later remove the older leaves and place in a cold frame at 40 degrees F. Then in early April force with fifty foot candle lighting for about a month.

You could set up a holiday schedule in the following manner. For Christmas sales, plant seed around the last week of April. For Valentine's Day, plant seed around the middle of June. For Easter, plant seed the first week of August. Using the same time table you could stagger production throughout the year and prepare for any holiday or occasion. Details for holiday production: after vernalization, set temperature at 65 degrees F, use 300-500 foot candles of light (sodium halide-high pressure) for nearly 18 hours a day.

Columneas or Goldfish Plants: Similar to hanging begonias: With excellent foliage and orange, red and yellow flowers each 3-4 inches in length, these plants make beautiful and exotic hanging baskets and will catch the eye of the customer. The plants have dark green foliage which is quite bushy and trails down over the edge of the container. The plants continue to bloom throughout the season.

How do you grow them? The pH should be around 6.0 with a medium which readily drains. The surface must be dry before you water again. Day temperatures can be anywhere from 70-90 degrees F. The plants require a lot of constant light. Fertilize with a constant feed which gives nitrogen at 150 ppm. The nitrogen level should be about the same as the potash level. One grower uses a 20-10-20 mixture. Very little pinching will be needed. An 8-inch hanging basket will require 5 plugs per basket. It takes about 14 or more weeks to have the basket market-ready. In the past a good supplier of this plant has been Aloha Exotics, 59-626 Akanoho PL, Haleaiwa, HI 96712.

The following is a list of some of the newest varieties which might tantalize the public. A supplier's address is also given for each variety. **PLEASE KEEP IN MIND THAT SUPPLIERS AND ADDRESSES CAN CHANGE.**

Arabella (Anthurium scherzeranum) - Twyford, 15245 Telegraph Rd, Santa Paula, CA 93060.
Lady Jane (Anthurium) - Oglesby Nursery, 3714 SW 52nd Ave, Hollywood, FL 33023.
Chantilly (Begonia) - Mikkelsens, Inc, P O Box 1536, Ashtabula, OH 44004.
Boaldi (Chrysanthenum) - Yoder Bros, P O Box 230, Barberton, OH 44203
Ruby (Cyclamen) - Daehnfeldt, P O Box 947, Albany, OR 97321.
Pastel Flame (Cyclamen) - Northrup King, 7500 Olsen Memorial Hwy, Golden Valley, MN 55427.

Alstroemeria: Also called Rosy Wings: This is a dwarf hybrid and is quite pretty. The plant flowers at about 8-10 inches in height after being held under cool conditions. Once the plant starts flowering, it continues do so for a long period of time. This makes it the ideal plant for the consumer. Warmer temperatures will cause the plant to stretch but you can control this by pinching back and by using smaller pot sizes. The normal pot size is six inches. This plant is quite sensitive to its nitrogen needs. Therefor, during the cooling period before blooming, use a fertilizer which has 400 ppm of nitrogen. After the cooling period use 200 ppm of nitrogen. This plant also doesn't like wet feet. Let it dry out slightly between waterings/feedings. Too little light will slow down the flowering process. Stems which have small growth or no blooms should be cut off.

If you start out in the fall, which would be logical, the first two months go like this. The rhizomes should be planted with at least two growing shoots showing. Use a fungicide the first week after you've planted - drench the medium and the pot with it. Keep at 55-60 degrees F, especially at night. The second month (probably November or December if you started in late September) the plants should be kept at 40 degrees F, and not less than 32 degrees F, for nearly six weeks. Again, before this cooling period, drench the medium with a fungicide and allow the plants to almost dry out.

If you're growing for Easter or Mother's Day, pull the plants out of the cooler (around January 23 if you planted in early October) and place them in a growing area at 60-70 degrees F days and 55 degrees F nights. They'll need lots of light during the daytime hours. Bad foliage should be removed. About 3 weeks later cut back 1/4 of the stems or shoots to the medium surface level. All other stems or shoots should be pinched back one-half. Two weeks later thin out those stems which didn't make it. And pinch halfway down the stems any new shoots. After this these floral stems should not be pinched back. Vegetative stems can be pinched back at will to make the plant more attractive. Four weeks later the plants should start flowering. And what a show they'll be! Customers will love them. Try a few and find out for yourself.

Campanula or Bellflower: Very compact, very bushy, very pretty! Use terminal cuttings if you have this plant in stock. This is another "long-day" plant like Alstroemeria and also needs 8-10 weeks of cool temperatures. The long days have a break at night where light is used from 10 at night to 2 in the morning. The long days are used right after you've finished forcing. Light required will be 3000 foot candles. After the roots have taken hold, grow at 40-50 degrees F for two weeks. This is the forcing period. Then grow at 65 degrees F until the plants have spread out and become full. After that keep the temperature at 55-58 degrees F until blooming time. Use fertilizer in the range of 5-10-5 or 10-15-10. Use a mild nutrient solution and irrigate with clean water between feedings. Some growers use the following growth regulators. Use a 2% solution of A-Rest as soon as you see the bud. The same can be done with B- Nine (about 3000 ppm). The plant has a pretty good shelf life, but don't allow it to dry out. The plant will not tolerate low light. The prettiest hybrid is name Karl Foerster. It has blue stars for flowers, and it captivate customers. But place direction cards on both Alstroemeria and Campanula because they will need care in the home.

Ornamental Peppers: They've been around a long time and you'd think they'd be like yesterday's cold soup. But not so. Not only ornamental peppers but all peppers are coming back with a vengeance! What's more, we now have more compact and bushier types to consider. They are easy to grow. They don't take long to grow. And they keep their fruit and color for a long period of time. The best cultivars around today are the ones with the small round or thin fruits. The first group include cultivars with the trade name of Fireball and Holiday Cheer. The latter group would include Holiday Flame, Red Missile, Hotbed Slim. All are immensely popular throughout the year but more so at Christmas.

Culture: Germinate the seed at 70 degrees F. Maintain high humidity for about two weeks. Then transplant the seedlings immediately - usually to 4-inch containers. Good drainage must be provided at a pH of 6.0 - 6.5. Fertilize with nitrogen in the nitrate form at 150-200 ppm. Fertilize with every plant irrigation but don't forget to flush at least once a week with plain water. When the fruit sets start lowering the fertilizer amounts. The plant will flower seven weeks after the seed is sown and fruit ten weeks after the seed is sown. It takes the fruit 3-4 weeks to ripen. After germination, the growing temperature will be around 63 degrees F in direct sunlight. Plants will fruit and stay in good shape for 3-4 weeks. The type of medium used isn't critical as long as good drainage is provided. Sell the plants when about one-half of their fruit is ripe.

Miniature Roses: Predicted to be the top crop in a few years! And will be selling as low as five dollars per pot! Already popular in Europe, these plants can be bought and kept until they lose their beauty. After that they can be thrown away and replaced with another - all year round. With such potential it's a good idea for you to look at the possibilities. But how do you grow them? Miniature roses are sensitive to proper amounts of light, water, fertilizer and medium mix. The best medium mix seems to be extra amounts of perlite, peat moss and vermiculite. Good drainage from this mixture helps to prevent root rot. The rooted plants are placed in cold storage and then potted as needed throughout the year. The plants are in full bloom 8 weeks after potting. Rooted plants are placed in 4 or 6-inch standard pots. Plants which are actively growing when received should be pinched back at the growing tips until the fifth set of leaves appear. It takes nearly ten weeks from that date to have them ready to sell. For fall/winter selling, keep the night temperature at 58 degrees F, days at 70 degrees F and less. Feed at a constant rate with nitrogen in the 120 ppm range.

For spring/summer the plants should be pinched off 6 weeks ahead of selling date. Night temperature is kept a little cooler than the day temperature of 80 degrees F. Use 25% more nitrogen than with winter plants. Extra watering will be needed for new plants for at least 2-3 weeks until the roots have formed. Keep the medium moist like a wrung-out sponge (We can't say it too often!). An ideal constant feed type fertilizer (like Osmocote) will have about 140 ppm of nitrogen. You can also use soluble fertilizer about every 8-9 days. The diseases are: Botrytis, downy mildew, powdery mildew. Use Ornalin, Zyban, or Milban to combat these diseases. Spider mites are sometimes a problem. Use preventative spraying to eliminate this pest. Some recent additions to varieties now available are: Nor'East Miniature roses under the trade names of Lavender Jade and Mountie.

CHAPTER 12

COMPUTERS, LIGHTS, CROP MODELLING, TISSUE CULTURE:

Computers for the Greenhouse: Why, Where, When? There's no point investing in computerization when your profit from such an expenditure won't offset the cost. Why substitute an expensive computer for a thermostat which has been doing a fairly good job up until now? As with any other business expenditure, computerization must justify itself. Ideally the cost of computerization must be paid back from **EXTRA PROFITS** within two years. But perhaps the temperatures in your greenhouse vary greatly from place to place. The thermostat doesn't give the true story. You could gain more control with a computer which monitors those various temperatures and keeps them in line with norms you've established. The computer can also keep a log of temperatures throughout the growing season. This history will come in handy in later seasons. When you get right down to it, temperature is the primary control.

But computers are capable of controlling much more than temperature ranges. Computerization can monitor light levels, carbon dioxide levels, cost of fuel, moisture levels in the various media, humidity levels - along with doing your daily accounting, shipping and receiving, payroll and business activities. In short, when you're ready computerization can make you more competitive and thereby make you more money. So you're thinking about it? Let's take a look. First what's needed is a computer which has complete environmental control, using a system of sensors, software, electronics and daily tabulation. He who controls the computer controls the crop. From where you sit at the computer you can see what's going on in the whole operation. You can also change what's going on. The computer will help through its sensors to keep all the different systems, such as heating, watering and vents, from conflicting with one another. The day will come when you may use crop modelling where you set up the ideal parameters for raising a crop quickly and economically. Even before that day arrives, once you set the computer for the conditions you want, that's the way conditions will remain day in and day out until you decide to change them. Thus you can time your crop with much more accuracy and watch your profits grow. The computer will tell you in advance when a piece of equipment is about to fail. This will give you time to repair or replace.

One necessary piece of equipment is a battery setup for the computer in case of power outages. If the power goes out, the computer will continue to run. Some growers have several computers as modular controllers. If one computer breaks down, the others take over. Then all you've lost is the data for that day in that particular computer. There are other benefits. Labor expenses are dramatically reduced. You'll be able to make better growing decisions from the data stored in the computer. You'll have more time to do things important to your marketing program. Cost? It depends upon the number of sensors or environmental controls you wish to install. Let's say your in Zone 5 (growing area). Multiply 5 times $2000 for large installations, 5 times $3000 for small installations. And get an estimate from your vendor. Once you've decided upon computerization and exactly what you want it to do for you, look for the following in the system you choose:

1. Must be flexible. Must be able to do its environmental job in addition to handling jobs like payroll, accounting, market predictions, word processing.
2. Must be durable. Particularly under greenhouse conditions.
3. Sensors must be accurate and able to be finely tuned.
4. Everything must work together - software, computer, all systems.
5. Future expansion must be built-in. System will work with add-ons.
6. Must give you the information you need for future crop predictions.
7. The supplier must furnish the following: technical help through the first year, be financially stable and able to furnish your needs for years to come, can acquaint you with software updates, can set up the entire system and start it up, provide you with the necessary training, supply telephone consultation when you need it.
8. Must be easy to learn and easy to use. No complications - simple and to the point.
9. Must have automatic phone dialing to alert you in emergencies.

So you're ready to buy? Just remember it takes time to learn a new computer setup no matter how user-friendly the computer is reputed to be. When you do buy, make certain you get much more disk space than you now need. Getting it now will be a lot cheaper than adding it on later. Software must be adaptable to common and botanical names. Software must be able to do discount pricing for different order sizes - this is needed for profitable wholesaling.

For those interested in an economical way to computerize, contact: IFAS Computer Support Office, Bldg 120, Room 201, University of Florida, Gainesville, FL 32611. These people have developed a system which controls as many as twenty devices for a moderate cost. The system incorporates the use of a personal home-sized computer. Not sophisticated of course, but good enough for small installations.

Lights: Only uniform consistent lighting is recommended: This means the light levels are as nearly equal as possible over a given area. From side to side and from length to length. If you have a moving light system, this will in a prescribed time give equal lighting to the given area. More importantly plants seem to do better with a moving system. Static or in-place lights are only for the hobbyist with a hundred square feet or so of growing space. Plants only use light when it reaches a certain level. Lighting brighter than this prescribed level will not make the plant perform any better. So there's no use in wasting energy. If the light isn't uniform the plants will grow in a non-uniform manner and will not all mature at the same time. This will lead to production and labor problems.

Light is measured in foot candles which is a measure more suitable to the human eye than it is to plants. At present the horticultural industry has been grossly neglected by manufacturers of lighting devices. So when you shop for lighting make sure you ask for a light distribution pattern which is produced by the entire gang of proposed lights. Don't listen to the salesman - he knows just about as much as you do, if not less. **INSPECT THE MANUFACTURER'S RESTRICTIONS AND WARRANTY CONDITIONS.** If you fail to use a lamp as instructed by the manufacturer, you not only endanger your crop and yourself but you may also invalidate your fire insurance if a fire should occur.

The crop itself will dictate the amount and kind of lighting it requires. Plants generally require between 500-600 foot candles. Remember this: light from a lamp loses its intensity as it travels - by as much as 70% for every foot of travel! This suggests that lamps must be closer to plants than hitherto recognized. For 40 watt/sq foot coverage, suspend the lamps 12-15 inches above the tops of the plants. Some power companies will now give rate discounts at off-peak periods for greenhouse growers. This can be a significant savings and is something well worth looking into. Lights can be used to good advantage during the winter months, on cloudy days, and for crops which require more (longer day) light to reach maturity.

Any lighting system you buy must be one which can stand up under the environment in which it is placed. In hydroponics, lighting has to stand up under moisture. Additionally the installation of lighting must take into consideration other mechanical and feeding/watering devices you have already installed. You wouldn't want a misting system to spray onto a hot lamp. One authority suggests you consider the 4th generation of metal halide lamps, specifically one named Pro- Arc. This lamp seems to have the features which most plants desire. Also this lamp is competitive in pricing, has variety and is of good quality and delivery. If you just want lamps which control the length of the day, when in effect you are lying to the plant, then high pressure sodium lamps will do.

What lamps to use? Well what plant are you growing? What are its lighting requirements? What kind of light did this plant get in its natural state? How much of that light is required for the plant's normal growing period? How much area of the plant bed will you have to light? Do you want to throw light on plants lying under a bench? If so, maybe you'd prefer a different setup. What kind of light does the plant prefer? **YOU MUST DETERMINE ITS SPECTRUM NEEDS.** If you use a tiered growing system, you'll have to design your lighting to reach all the plants. Above all choose the correct reflectors. Ones which reflect outward and not back onto the lamps. Use a good tracking system for moving lamps. Sunshine Bar Solar Tracker is recommended by one authority as being designed specifically for greenhouse commercial use. One more thing: **DON'T GO INTO THE GROWING AREA WHEN THE LIGHTS ARE ON!** If you must go in, do so just before the lights are turned on - not after they've been burning for a while. **HOT LAMPS ARE TOO DANGEROUS TO BE AROUND!**

Crop Modelling and Environmental Control: Where computers shine! We all believe that computerization can help control greenhouse environment but that's just the beginning of what computers can do for us. Since climate control is attended by a great number of variables, climate control would be fertile territory for the computer which is particularly suited to this sort of calculation.

So what is crop modelling? And where does the computer fit into the picture? A specific plant which you intend to grow is studied daily as it grows. Its growth patterns and measurements are relayed to a computer which automatically stores them away for future reference. At the same time, temperature, humidity, and electrical conductivity in the nutrient and the medium are observed. These readings are conveyed to the computer. Everything which influences the growth of the plant is given to the computer. Under idealized conditions the computer can get a dynamic grasp of what's going on and store it for future use. This entails having an actual plant (model) being under daily scrutiny. Not only is the daily change in height being noted but also the size and number of leaves, the size and number of fruit and the general health and appearance of the plant. With such dynamic modelling an alert grower can be on the cutting edge of competition. He can get the computer to provide optimal growth environment for his crops and thus produce better crops faster and at a given time.

Needless to say the computer must be linked with the general environmental control of the greenhouse and growing areas. This might and probably will entail the use of another main computer which controls the environment. Our modelling computer would then instruct the main computer to direct greenhouse controls to enable crop production at the most optimal level that would match the model instruction stored in the model computer's memory banks.

It's getting to the point where we control everything in the chosen environment. It's not science fiction; it's already here. Now computers are being programmed to control diseases and are able to know when it's the best time to apply corrective measures such as fungicide sprays. Best of all a well-designed computer system can quickly pay back its costs in energy savings alone, thus freeing management for other tasks like marketing and increased production. Though growers already know that Botrytis control is implemented by having sanitary conditions, many times it's not cost effective to carry through with the implementation. Plants become too congested; dead leaves fall and accumulate. And there's no time to clean them up. Botrytis spores love this sort of accumulation and will rapidly make a home in it. What do you have in a case like this? A recipe for losses! But with computer control sensors can detect and count the number of Botrytis spores in the air and then convey this information to the computer which already has an inner established parameter for how many spores can be allowed. When that parameter has been reached, the computer can turn on the proper fungicide spray units and get rid of the Botrytis.

Sounds fanciful? Wishful thinking? Not really. It's just a matter of time before such control is possible. Most growers already acknowledge the computer as useful for environmental control. For those growers who are already using computerized environmental control, some interesting features abound. One grower can now go home for the weekend because he has a portable computer which he takes with him. By using a modem he can telephone the greenhouse computer and see what's going on. Or he can make changes in various environmental parameters. He can also have a pager which calls him when anything goes wrong. But even if there is something wrong, he can still stay home. He can make his changes from home.

Tissue Culture: The future may be very bright! After you get beneath the technical language used by genetic engineers, limitless prospects for plants of all sorts of adaptability may be on the menu of the future. This includes plants with drought resistance, herbicide resistance, hybrids designed for specific uses. But don't get too excited. There is still much to be discovered before all of this becomes a reality. So far only a handful of genes which can be useful have been found. And only a handful of plant tissues with protoplasts are known which can generate entire plants.

Further, we have low frequencies of known techniques for activating those tissue cells. What's more, very little is known about how a gene will act when introduced into a plant cell. Research has recently exploded based on the idea of cloning. This theory expresses the idea that each cell in a plant is capable of regenerating a new and completely identical plant. This theory is called totipotency. Lately the theory has been proven correct. Getting it to work is another matter.

What are the requirements for tissue culture?
(1) You must have a totally aseptic condition. This means everything connected with the culture must be absolutely germ and bacteria free. This includes the laboratory.
(2) The medium being used must be acceptable. The medium includes nutrients, growth regulators and pH control. Agar, a gel, is often used as the base.
(3) The type of explant must be considered - using different cells from different plants.
(4) The temperature range for successful experimentation is 22-28 degrees Centigrade. Hours of light and dark will vary from culture to culture.
(5) Transferring cultures depends a lot on the technician. If he can separate the cells which will respond in a way he anticipates, his chances for success will be much better.

Many applications of the above are now in progress. **CLONING** is widely used in horticultural centers. Orchids are a fine example of this art. Most orchids you now see have originated from meristem cultures which clone more orchids. Meristem is a group of plant cells which have the ability to sub-divide and grow. Usually a shoot meristem is used - these are cells from the shoot area of the plant. The **CALLUS** is a group of growing cells hanging in a liquid medium. Some uses for a callus culture are to test for toxicities which may affect the plant. The theory is that if the callus reacts to, say a herbicide, then the grown plant will also react in a similar manner. Some useful products can be induced from a callus - such as morphinane, caffeine, nicotine and oils for cosmetics. Mutant selection is based on the callus. Also **PROTOPLASTS** are very useful products which can be obtained from the callus. Protoplasts are cells with their cell walls taken away. Using the technique of fusion, a technician can fuse a tomato to a potato and have the resultant plant. **HAPLOIDS** are useful in hybrid programs. **EMBRYO RESCUE** is used for seed viability, seed dormancy problems, and some interplay between host-pathogens. This last technique is somewhat complex.

THE FUTURE? Genetic engineers who can now isolate fragments of DNA will, in time, "create" plants with the characteristics needed by society. With the combination of molecular biologists, tissue culture and cell transformation technicians, there may come a time when all of us will have to stretch our imagination just to barely comprehend.

THE END? Believe it or not, there is more. No one book can cover a field so vast as hydroponics. But this book does cover a lot of territory. This book gives you a detailed birds-eye view which can stand you in good stead as you go about the business of growing plants. This book does, for the first time, show a way for the amateur to begin in a field where information is difficult to come by. The amateur can start out in the "crude" fashion related in

Section One. If he so desires he need go no further than Section One. But if he really wants to grow and also become commercially successful, he will venture into Section Two and apply the applicable concepts to his own situation. What about the future? It has only just begun. The world will rapidly turn toward raising food, plants and flowers the hydroponic way. Most of it will be done in the ways which have been described in this book. In the future, there will be few problems with poor soil, dwindling water supplies, acid rain. And there will be demand for new products, for drugs such as belladonna, ipeca, ephedrine, digitalis. It will be a large future for the hydroponist. But for now you have the help you need. The rest is up to you.

In parting, here are some suppliers:

Dean's Greenhouses, 3984 Porter Rd, Westlake, OH 44145 - has cuttings for geraniums, etc.

Earl D Small, 6901 49th St N, Pinellas Park, FL 33565 - seedlings and cuttings for gloxinia, begonia, etc.

Granger Gardens, 1060 Wilbur Rd, Medina, OH 44256 - blooming African Violets - not recommended for beginners.

Lindemann Laboratories, 61 Brown Rd, Ithaca, NY 14850 - Boston fern, others - rooted from tissue culture.

Mums by Paschke, 12286 East Main St, Northeast, PA 16428 - cuttings.

The Lehman Gardens, 420 10th St SW, Faribault, MN 55021 - Mums - cuttings.

Sunny Border Nurseries, 1708 Kensington Rd., Kensington, CT 06037 - herbs, plants. (Herbs are also easy to grow from seed.)

Chapin Watermatics, 740 Water St, Watertown, NY 13601 - automatic watering and feeding lines and hoses, etc.

Florists Mutual Ins Co, 500 St Louis St, Edwardsville, IL 62025 - greenhouse insurance. Absolutely essential!

ALL ADDRESSES ARE SUBJECT TO CHANGE. CHECK WITH YOUR SUPPLIER IF ANY OF THESE ADDRESSES SEEM INCORRECT. SUPPLIERS OFTEN HAVE THE LATEST DATA ON HAND.

Plus the following: If you don't want a visit from your state's environmental department, be sure to do the following. **USE ALL CHEMICALS AND PESTICIDES IN A SAFE MANNER.** Follow the manufacturer's instructions to the letter. Make certain the items you use are registered with your state as being legal to use. Protect yourself and your employees with the proper clothing. If you don't do these things, you may find yourself facing steep fines and maybe some government paid vacation time. The recommended clothing for those who work with pesticides are: both long-sleeved shirts and long pants or coveralls. The shirt must button to the neck. Wear gloves and boots. Do not tuck shirt sleeves inside gloves or pants inside boots. Surgical gloves are preferred to cloth because cloth soaks up the pesticide. Boots must be waterproof or eventually the pesticide will seep through. Wear head covering when working under overhead plants. **PROTECT SKIN ENTRY FROM PESTICIDES AT ALL TIMES!** Do this even after "safe" time has elapsed and remember that some workers will be more sensitive than others to pesticides and herbicides.

The EPA is getting into the act. This organization is worried about the runoff from greenhouses. You should be worried too. Because if a neighbor's water supply becomes contaminated and he can prove your runoff caused it, you are going to have a problem. Those of you who already have recirculating nutrient systems won't have much to worry about. Those who don't will have to change their way of doing things. The EPA will be interested in any insecticides or fungicides you use. Extra care in storage and use will have to be taken. Even if you follow the label instructions on the chemicals you use, you can still be held liable for contamination of ground water. Consequently you must find ways to avoid such contamination. This groundwater controversy has been going on for some time. Many towns and cities are becoming increasingly more alert and aggressive when confronting this issue.

You don't have to go to Japan or California to find a commercial hydroponic operation. Just look in the Yellow Pages, under Greenhouses, Growers or Nurseries. Most American growers are using hydroponic techniques which now-a-days means anything but soil.

A new biotechnological company engaged in tissue culture is applying what it knows to creating vegetables never seen before. This company will be able to provide "designer" vegetables, customized to your wishes, within a short period of time. Ever wonder why large companies with big budgets fail in their attempts at hydroponics? The main factor lacking in such operations: a single-minded desire to succeed no matter what anyone else says. Yes you need some money but not a whole lot. What you really need is determination to do your own thing!

WHAT OTHERS ARE DOING:

Hyroponic Hay: A dairy farmer at Dowlingville in South Australia knows how to keep his dairy herd well fed during the summer months when rain and feed are scarce. He uses barley grown hydroponically as a supplemental feed. This not only keeps his herd healthy but also gives him premium prices from higher grades of butter fat in the milk he sells. Why barley as opposed to other grains? The farmer thinks this grain germinates better than other grains and is easier to grow with hydroponics. His favorite brand of seed is called Schooner. The barley seed is first soaked in water for twelve hours. Then the grain is moved to polystyrene trays which measure 35.5 inches by 12 inches by 4 inches. The farmer uses sixty trays a day to feed 55 cows. Each tray stays in his hydroponic shed for seven days. The process is somewhat like growing alfalfa sprouts which are sold in supermarkets in the United States. Requirements for growing the barley are a temperature of 45 degrees F and a humidity level of 75%. Barley does best with 16 hours of light. For awhile the farmer used supplemental lighting but he doubts the extra lighting is worth the added cost.

Problems with summer heat (when the fodder is needed most) are overcome with a sprinkler system which sprays the walls and the ceiling on the outside. Also a wet pad cooling system helps to keep the temperature down. While in the trays, the barley gets watered three times a day, with nutrient mix the first four days and water thereafter. This combination of feeding and watering gives the highest level of protein available in the grass feed. The hydroponic fertilizer mix consists of the following: a total of 1200 Grams which includes 100 grams of chelated iron and 800 grams of calcium nitrate. This is all mixed together in a 600 gallon tank. The mixture lasts for a little over two months. The shed in which the farmer places the trays measures 40 ft by 15 ft by 9 ft. The trays are placed on racks about 30 feet long and seven tiers high. When the grass is ready to be fed to the cows, the trays are taken outside and tipped over into the feed bin. The farmer is thinking about setting up this operation on a conveyor belt. Seed at one end and feed at the other!

According to the information we have, the shed has walls and a ceiling which are coated with 50 mm of sprayed polurethane which is designed to keep the temperature around 45 degrees F. Evidently light comes through windows and/or skylights. Otherwise the barley wouldn't grow. This idea might work well in the United States and Canada - if you experimented with shade cloth to get the proper amount of light. You might have a difficult time getting the temperature down in the average greenhouse - especially in the summer.

But you could still grow the other three seasons and supplement with other feed you might have on hand. This idea would preserve the other feed you have and hold it for the months when you wouldn't be able to meet the temperature requirements. Perhaps if you used tier shelving you would be better off doing it like an A-frame in order for all the plants to get light.

Hydroponics in Israel: Most of Israel is arid and has little water available for crop production. This has given rise to the use of hydroponics on a large scale, more so percentage-wise than for any other country. Also the proximity of the European market for cut flowers such as carnation, roses and chrysanthemums has given a sharp rise in hydroponic usage. Lately a large expanding market for foliage has come into existence.

NFT in the ordinary sense isn't used. A method called Ein-Gedi is used instead. In this method the plant's roots are immersed in a deep flowing solution. A fully developed mist is allowed to develop in the space between the light cap and the surface of the solution. This space is completely filled with mist. In some cases the entire trough is full of mist with no liquid at all flowing through the trough. The roots have ready access to oxygen and food. Plant growth is effectively controlled by varying the ratios of the mist with the nutrient solution. Aside from Ein-Gedi, sand and tuff cultures are the leading methods used in Israel. Tuff culture is foremost in some parts of the country. Tuff is volcanic ash used for the planting medium. Tuff holds water and air, making a perfect medium. Since drip irrigation is one of the foremost feed and watering mechanisms used in Israel, tuff culture allows for its continuous use without injury to root systems.

Tuff contains permanent as well as variable ion charges; so care must be taken to have the correct pH and nutritional balance. This includes the balance between tuff and the solution. Growers believe in daily fertilization. Therefor leaching must be done now and then with large doses of water in order to prevent salt accumulation. European buyers don't like the tuff medium; so some growers are now using expanded clay, an artificial gravel which is manufactured from clay and a lot of heat. Sand culture is used along the Mediterranean Sea where climatic conditions are not as severe as in the interior. This is "dune" sand - it has relatively large particles and a very low ability to hold ions or water. Sand culture of this kind is responsible for Israel's creation of drip irrigation, because the sand has to be moist at all times. This is especially true when using salt water. The growers of Israel are among the very few who have learned how to use salt water with plants. The secret is to use frequent applications in a trickle irrigation pattern. Both water and nutrients are fed at predetermined rates, depending upon the chemistry of the sand and the needs of the crop. This is all automated; therefor larger crops can be expected. Cabutz is made from manure which has been composted and then watered to make a slurry. This mixture is run over a screen which separates the liquid from the solids. The liquid becomes fertilizer; the solids become a medium for plants. Some think that cabutz may be the answer for economy as well as for quality. With ideas like these, it's no wonder the growers of Israel demand attention. Their climate and soil places them at the front line of hydroponic development.

Hydroponics in Japan: The rise of hydroponics in Japan rests upon the U.S. Army's use of hydroponics in Chofy, Tokyo right after World War II and also upon the increase in vegetable injury from micro-organisms in the soil. Today most of Japan's hydroponics is done with NFT or sand/gravel techniques. Using bio-technical approaches such as posed by hydroponics, the Japanese have come up with newer and more productive plants such as the huge tomato plant shown in recent years at the Tsukiba Expo. This plant had produced over 10,000 large fruits! It was done with extra lighting techniques. Their number one nutrient flow technique involves slabs of styrofoam floating on the nutrient solution. Urethane cubes with implanted seedlings are inserted into tapered holes in the styrofoam "rafts". These slabs are about 1 1/2 to 2 inches in thickness, thin enough to allow the roots of the new plant to reach the nutrient solution below. The slabs are placed next to each other and form one continuous floating platform from one end of the greenhouse to the other. Thus a crop can be planted at one end of the greenhouse and harvested at the other! Small pumps aerate the liquid under the "rafts"; this gives oxygen to the root systems above. Since the rafts are tightly fitted to each other, the root systems are kept in the dark where they can flourish.

Fruiting vegetables are grown in sand or gravel and, in more recent cases, in rockwool cubes and slabs. Many Japanese growers are turning to the solid media - these are not usually interconnected and do not easily transmit disease. Japanese growers like extra artificial lighting which gives continuous growing without regard to the weather. HYPONICS is the name of a popular system where gravel pots are set inside troughs or beds and a nutrient solution is allowed to flow intermittently through the beds. Similar to the ebb-flow technique discussed earlier, the solution is allowed to rise to the top of the pots and is then drained away. The plant is seeded directly into the pot. Air is constantly mixed with the nutrient solution as it leaves the tap. The M-method is the styrofoam raft explained above. SANDPONICS is a system which uses drip irrigation instead of the usual flooding techniques practiced in sand/gravel beds. In this method the beds are 3 inches deep and 24 inches wide. The system allows for gravity feed and aeration. Most plants are planted/seeded directly into the bed. It now seems that the Japanese are currently more interested in recirculating (closed system) nutrient techniques than they are with sand or other media. Hydroponics is now well established in Japan, particularly for vegetables such as cucumbers, melons, tomatoes, lettuce, honeworts, strawberries, radish sprouts, leeks and green Welsh onions. One of the most remarkable applications of hydroponics is a computerized NFT system in the Daiei supermarket which is located in Funabashi City at the Lalaport Shopping Center, one of the largest in Asia. Starting from scratch (seed!) in the back of the store, the product makes its way as it grows until it reaches the customer up front. Only four technicians control the entire process.

One technician operates the computer, the others tend the crop. Inside a 70 square yard laboratory, glass windows allow you to see large heads of lettuce in plastic beds, ready for market. The computer controls temperature, light, humidity, nutrient, carbon dioxide and water. Seeds are grown in canisters filled with water. When their primary leaves begin to show, the technician place them into one inch cubes of rockwool (horticultural or agricultural). The plants are kept separate from the main growing room until they have about five leaves. The seedling is then plugged into a hole on the plastic board where it will grow until harvest time. With all its plants now intact, the board is taken to the main growing area and allowed to float on a nutrient bath solution. Almost like a conveyor belt, the board floats and moves upon the nutrient solution. What normally took 80 days or more to get to harvest now takes about 35 days.

Though the system was copied from similar ones in Denmark and the U.S., the Daiei supermarket uses only artificial lights to grow crops. Such systems in other countries use both artificial and natural light. This combination of lighting is becoming more popular in the U.S. With artificial lights only, electricity comprises half of the total costs of production. Even with the higher costs of electrical usage, the vegetables grown are sold at only 2-4% higher price than those grown in traditional ways. It seems Japanese housewives don't mind paying extra if they're certain they're receiving highly nutritious, clean lettuce. The supermarket grows five different kinds of lettuce and is considering other vegetables for the process.

This is the only known supermarket which has gone to such drastic means to insure quality to its customers. Two large Japanese companies are looking for ways to improve on the system and export it to interested parties. This kind of hydroponics is very useful in a country which has limited land space for agriculture. Some Japanese growers think the system can be accommodated to multi-story buildings.

The Netherlands: Europe's top contender for output and ideas: We hear a lot about competition from the Netherlands, especially in regard to cut flowers which are exported to the United Sates. But the Dutch are very competitive, at home and abroad. Being a small country with little land to spare, greenhouse construction is at an all-time high. The recipe for hydroponic success in the Netherlands is, like anywhere else, to have a good grower. That grower must know his market, must look at new developments in plant culture, must like to take risks, and must along with his family enjoy working in tropical conditions for long hours.

The Dutch keep their greenhouses producing all year-round with some heating in the winter months. Not much cooling is needed in the summer because the climate is relatively mild due to influences from the Gulf Stream. One of the problems encountered is water quality, especially in the Western part of the country. Western growers use large catchment tanks for rain water because well water is too saline or otherwise unfit for plants. Control is a key word in a Dutch grower's vocabulary. Control to the Dutch includes computers. They are so conscious of computers that they have begun marketing their computer programs to other countries. As one grower puts it, it's a lot easier and far more cost-effective to control a problem than to let it get out of hand before doing something about it. Control includes, among other things, ways to conserve energy. Some of these ways are the use of root-zone heating, using plant cultivars which are more adapted to cooler climates, having energy curtains (discussed under blanketing), and using methods which insure greenhouse covers are airtight. With the advent of hydroponics, Dutch growers first utilized NFT techniques but now a large percentage of them are using rockwool. This medium can be used for several years when it is sterilized between uses. Since rockwool is not biodegradable, a problem arises for its final disposal. So far the only solution which has come to mind is to use the spent rockwool to repair dikes which keep out the sea. It's in the use of computers where Dutch growers have advanced the most. The daily climate inside their greenhouses changes rapidly. Computers are almost a necessity to help control these changes.

There are relatively few spots throughout the world where daily climate changes occur so rapidly. And only a few growers in any of these areas can afford computers of the sort the Dutch envision. The leading manufacturers of climate controls come from the Netherlands. Some of the companies are Hoogendoorn Automasisering, Van Vliet, Brinkman B.V., V & V Nordland Agro Products and Priva BV. Small systems cost in US dollars from $5,000 to $10,000 while larger systems run over $50,000. These prices do not include the extras such as sensors, valves and cables. Dutch greenhouse computer systems endeavor to control each of the following: carbon dioxide concentration, heating system, ventilation, humidity, air temperature, incoming sunlight. These are controlled by sensors which are placed at appropriate intervals throughout the greenhouse. Nutrient levels, moisture content, temperature of the medium are also sensed and their levels relayed back to the computer which orders any necessary corrections. The main problem with greenhouse climate control is software. More pertinent software needs to be developed. Though the software now in use has performed satisfactorily it lags somewhat behind what is preferred. The next market thrust for the Dutch is to compose better software.

it lags somewhat behind what is preferred. The next market thrust for the Dutch is to compose better software.

Saudi Arabia: Hydroponics in the middle of the desert.

At Riyadh in Saudi Arabia, an American company and its crew set up an 18 acre greenhouse complex which they continue to service and monitor. Since water is more valuable than oil to the Saudis and since the water they have is poor in quality, the Americans had a difficult problem to overcome. With an average rainfall of 8 inches per year, if the Saudis want to grow vegetables they have to rely on ground water which is loaded with salt. But as poor as the water is, the Saudis hope it doesn't run out. The weather is hot and dry. The average yield for vegetables in the field is about 5 tons for each acre used (85,000 acres in all). Yet in the greenhouse at Riyadh, the American company gets more than 200 tons for each acre planted! No wonder the Saudis are impressed and urging the Americans on to higher achievements.

One of the reasons hydroponics is making such a good show for itself in Saudi Arabia is the fact that water goes a lot further inside a greenhouse than out in the field. Most of the water used in the greenhouse is for evaporative cooling. With all these restrictions, crops are limited to those which are economical to grow. Basically these crops are tomatoes, some lettuce, peppers and cucumbers. The complex at Riyadh, known as Ibrahim Abunayan Farms, also grows cut flowers which do quite well in an artificial environment and which are in great demand. The last we heard, the complex had been in production nearly eight years. The American company brought in its own 5-gallon upright plastic bags and used a medium composed of peat-lite and sand/gravel obtained from the local area. In order to maintain the complex's profitability, the cooling system had to be more than adequate and everyone had to be on his toes. Picking the right cultivars was another important task. Choosing a plan to schedule plantings, feeding, and the how and when of implementing disease and insect control were all delicate matters in the desert climate.

You might not think insects would be a problem. But Middle Eastern countries harbor huge insect populations. Most insects, including whitefly, love dry heat. Whitefly is the most harmful because it carries a virus which infects tomato and cucumber plants. In order to slow down the fly's activities, the American company used a filter which was attached to each cooling pad. Another problem arose. Evaporative pads don't last long in the desert. They soon become clogged with the salt in the water. The Americans found it more economical to replace these pads instead of using more expensive water obtained through desalinization. The complex now uses a highly absorbent plastic pad which seems to do the job quite well.

APPENDIX: Bibliography:

Douglas, James, ADVANCED GUIDE TO HYDROPONICS, Viking Press. ISBN 0-7207-1571-7. Specific and to the pont.

Douglas, J. Sholto, HYDROPONICS: THE BENGAL SYSTEM. Oxford Univ. Press, ISBN 0-19-560566-7. The system on which our modified plan in Section One is based.

Gooze, Joseph, THE HYDROPONIC WORKBOOK: A GUIDE TO SOILLESS GARDENING, Rocky Top Publ., ISBN 0-937317-00-4.

Harris, Dudley, HYDROPONICS, GROWING PLANTS WITHOUT SOIL, David and Charles, North Pomfret, VT 05053.

Joiner, Jasper N, FOLIAGE PLANT PRODUCTION, Prentice-Hall, Englewood Cliffs, NJ 07632. Very thorough and a must for those raising foliage.

Jones, J Benton, A GUIDE FOR THE HYDROPONICS AND SOILLESS CULTURE GROWER, Timber Press, 9999 SW Wilshire, Portland, OR 97225.

Nelson, Paul V., GREENHOUSE OPERATIONS AND MANAGEMENT, Prentice Hall, ISBN 0-835-2583-8. How to plan for maximum efficiency.

Pierce, John H., GREENHOUSE GROW HOW, Scribner, ISBN 0-918730-01-5.

Resh, Howard, HYDROPONIC FOOD PRODUCTION, Woodbridge Press Publishing Co, PO Box 6189, Santa Barbara, CA 93160. Very good supplementary text for those raising vegetables.

Saunby, T, SOILLESS CULTURE, Transatlantic Arts, Inc., Levittown, NY.

Savage, Adam J, PLANNING MANUAL FOR COMMERCIAL HYDROPONIC GROWERS and HYDROPONICS WORLDWIDE, Optimal Systems Corp., 400 Hobron Lane, Suite 3502, Honolulu, HI, 96815-1209. ISBN 0-934495-01-7/ - MASTER GUIDE TO PLANNING PROFITABLE HYDROPONIC GREENHOUSE OPERATIONS. Same address. Very worthwhile text to have on hand.

Sutherland, Struan, HYDROPONICS FOR EVERYONE, Hyland Austrialia Intl Spec Bk, ISBN 0-908090-94.

Taylor, James D., GROW MORE NUTRITIOUS VEGETABLES, Parkside Pr Publ, ISBN 0-911585-25-7.

Wilson, James W., "Raise Vegetables as Cash Crops," Mother Earth News, January/February 1983, pp 176-7.

Trade magazines: AMERICAN VEGETABLE GROWER, 37841 Euclid Ave, Willoughby, OH 44094. Devoted mostly to field crops and some greenhouse operations.

AMERICAN FRUIT GROWER AND GREENHOUSE GROWER, 37841 Euclid Ave, Willoughby, OH 44094.

THE GROWER, 49 Doughty Street, London WCIN-2BR, England. PUBLISHERS, LIKE PEOPLE, DO CHANGE THEIR ADDRESSES FROM TIME TO TIME. WE HAVE TRIED TO GET AS ACCURATE AN ADDRESS AS POSSIBLE. ALSO A BOOK MAY NO LONGER BE IN PRINT EVEN THOUGH THE PUBLISHER IS STILL AT THE SAME ADDRESS AS ABOVE.

GREENHOUSES AND HYDROPONIC SUPPLIERS: The following are listed alphabetically by state for quick acces sto your area. Most of these handle all kinds of supplies, including greenhouse structures and hydroponic systems. A few will be limited in what they offer, but most will be able to handle your needs. CAUTION: Do not be quick to buy someone's "hydroponic system". Make certain it fits your needs.

****

Far North Garden Supply
2834 Boniface Pkwy
Anchorage, AK 88504

Far North Garden Supply
300 Susitna Avenue
Wasilla, AK 99654

Mission Gardens
1525 E. Main St.
Mesa, AZ 85203

Sea of Green
4340 N. 7th Avenue
Phoenix, AZ 85013

American Hydroponics
286 S "G" St
Arcata, CA 95521

Applied Hydroponics
3135 Kerner Blvd
San Rafael, CA 94901

Foothill Hydropon
10705 Burbank Blvd
N. Hollywood, CA 91601

Greentrees
2469 S Santa Fe Ave
Vista, CA 92084

Honeyacre Corp
21885 Hwy 6, Ste 2
Apple Valley, CA 92307

Pure Food Co.
3385 El Camino Real
Santa Clara, CA 95051

Westmark Co.
3529 Touriga Dr.
Pleasanton, CA 94556

Mrs. Greenjeans
5020 D. Federal Blvd
Englewood, CA 80110

Hydro-Gardens
P.O. Box 9707
Colorado Springs, CO 80932

Nexus Corp
10983 Leroy
Northglenn, CO 80233

Growing Experience
1901 NW 18th, Bldg E
Pompano Beach, FL 33069

Speedling, Inc.
P.O. Box 220
Sun City, FL 33586

Worm's Way - Florida
4402 N. 56th St.
Tampa FL 33610

Southern Lts/Hydropon
6200 Buford Hwy 1-C
Norcross, GA 30071

Worm's Way - Indiana
3151 S. Hwy 446
Blooington, IN 47401

Chicago Indoor Sup
297 N. Barrington Rd
Streamwood, IL 60107

W W Granger
5959 W. Howard St.
Chicago, IL 60648

J-M Trading
241 Frontage Rd
Burr Hill, IL 60521

JPA
P.O. Box 60185
West Chicago, IL

Sto-Cote Products
P.O. Drawer 310
Richmond, IL 60071

Vaughan's
5300 Katherine Ave.
Downers Grove, IL 60515

Green Circle Hydrop
6904 W. 105th St.
Overland Park, KS 66212

New Earth
9810 Taylorsville Rd
Louisville, KY 40299

Caves Enterprises
Rt 4, Box 91
Hammond, LA 70401

Almac Plastics Inc.
6311 Erdman Ave.
Baltimore, MD 21205

Bramen Co.
P.O. Box 70
Salem, MA 01970

Conrad Fafard (Peat)
P.O. Box 790
Agawam, MA 01001

Griffin Greenhouse
P.O. Box 36
Tewksbury, MA 01876

Ken Bar Inc.
24 Gould Street
Reading, MA 01867

Worm's Way - MA
1200 Millbury St.
Worchester, MA 01607

Leckler's Inc.
13001 Telegraph Rd.
LaSalle, MI 48145

Clyde Smith & Sons
8285 Newburgh
Westland, MI 48185

Superior Growers Sup
29217 Seven Mile Rd
Livonia, MI 48152

Hydroponic Garden Ctr
2500 University Ave. W.
St. Paul, MN 55114

A H Hummert Seed
2746 Chouteau Ave
St. Louis, MO 63103

Stuppy, Inc.
P.O. Box 12456
N. KS City, MO 64116

Worm's Way - Missouri
2063 Concourse Dr.
St. Louis, MO 63146

Horticultural Supply
409 N. Saddle Creek Rd.
Omaha, NE 66131

Astro-Packing Inc.
100 Thomas Rd, N.
Hawthorne, NJ 07507

Brady Mfg.
RD 4, Box 134
Jackson, NJ 08527

132

GREENHOUSES AND SUPPLIERS, Continued

X S Smith, Inc.
P.O. Drawer X
Red Bank, NJ 07701

E. Holtzer Inc.
P.O. Box 1250   07632
Englewood Cliffs, NJ

Albuerque Hydro
5030 Southern Ave, SE
Albuerque, NM 87108

Agro Organics Industries
151-23 34th Ave
Flushing, NY 11354

Moran Harris Co
60 Saginaw Dr. #A
Rochester, NY 14623

M.A.H.
175-G Commerce Dr
Hauppauge, NY 11788

Fred Reeve Inc.
132 Sound Ave.
Riverhead, NY 11901

Carolina Hydro Supply
P.O. Box 964
Cornelius, NC 28031

Hendrix & Dial, Inc.
P.O. Box 648
Greenville, NC 27835

Pro-Gro Products
P.O. Box 1945 (Rootcube)
Elizabeth City, NC 27905

Reddick Fumigants
P.O. Box 391
Williamson, NC 27892

Van Winderden Greenhouse
4078 Haywood Rd
Horse Shoe, NC 28742

B F G Supply
14500 Kinsman Rd
Burton, OH 44021

CropKing Inc.
P.O. Box 310
Medina, OH 44258

Mellingers
2310 S. Range Rd
N Lima, OH 44452

Rough Brothers Inc.
P.O. Box 16010
Cincinnati, OH 45216

Smithers-Oasis Co
P.O. Box 118 (Rootcubes)
Kent, OH 44240

Suncor Systems
P.O. Box 11116
Portland, OR 97211

American Agriculture
9220 SE Stark
Portland, OR 97216

E. C. Geiger
Rt 63 Box 285
Harleysville, PA 19438

Geo K Groff, Inc.
224 Maple Ave
Bird-In-Hand, PA 17505

New Earth Center
139 Northcreek Blvd
Goodlettsville, TN 37072

Chas A. Cook
208 E Oak St
Weatherford, TX 76806

Growers International
P.O. Box 10
Schulenerg, TX 78956

Texas Growers Supply
5990 N Sam Houston Pkwy E
Humble, TX 77396

E-Z Grow Gardens
4655 Brookwood
Salt Lake City, UT 84117

Virginia Hydropon
368 Newtown Rd #105
Virginia Beach, VA 23462

Green Thumb Gardening
P.O. Box 235
Underhill, VT 05489

Discount Garden Ctr.
14109 E. Sprague, Ste 5
Spokane, WA 99216

Future Garden Supply
11522 Canyon Road
Puyallup, WA 98373

Dramm Corp
P.O. Box 528
Manitowoc, WI 54220

Modine Mfg (Heaters)
1500 Dekoven Ave
Racine, WA 53401

CANADIAN SUPPLIERS

Garden Friendly Products
201-A 7889-132nd St.
Surrey, BC V3W 4N2

Multicrop Industries
5307 Pat Bay Hwy
Victoria, BC V8Y 1S9

Canadian Hydrogardens
411 Book Rd, West
Ancaster, Ont L0G 3L1

Homegrown Halide/Hydropnics
2717 Weston Rd
Weston ON M9M 2R4
  - Lights

Frank's Magic Crops, Inc.
480 Guelph Line
Burlington, Ont L7R 3M1

FRAPA Plastique Inc.
405 Eitheenth Ave.
Lacine, Quebec H8S 3R1
  -Lights

Bright Lights
2215 Walkley
Montreal, Quebec K4B 2JR

Lambert Peat Moss, Inc.
Riviere-Oelle, Quebec
G0L 2C0

Racine Sans Sol
755 rue Racine
Racine, Quebec G1R 2Y6

MISCELLANEOUS

Grass machine animal feeding system:

Richard Matherson
7671 Hanson Dr.
Oakland, CA 94611

For a very tough hail resistant woven poly plastic, send SASE with 3 22 cent stamps to:

Northern Greenhouse
Sales, Box 42
Neche, ND 58265

For expert tissue and nutrient analysis, write:

Dept. of Horticultural Sciences
Texas A & M University
College Station, TX 77843-2133

For information on computer products:

Green Air Products
P.O. Box 1318
Gresham, OR 97030

SUPPLEMENTAL LIGHTING

Diamond Lights
628 Lindaro St.
San Rafael, Ca 94901

Worm's Way - FL
4402 N 56th St.
Tampa, FL 33610

Chicago Indoor Garden
297 N. Barrington Rd
Streamwood, IL 60107

Worm's Way - IN
3151 S Hwy 446
Bloomington, IN

Worm's Way - MA
1200 Millnury St.
Worchester, MA 01607

Worm's Way - MO
2063 Concourse Dr
St. Louis, MO 63146

Lumenarc Lighting
37 Fairchild Place
W Caldwell, NJ 07006

Albuquerque Hydro
5030 Southern Ave SE
Albuquerque, NM 87108

Vary Industries
P.O. Box 248
Lewiston, NY 14092

American Agruicult
9220 SE Stark
Portland, OR 97216

Future Carden Sup
11522 Canyon Rd
Puyallup, WA 98373

Green Gardens
12748 NE Bell Red Rd
Bellevue, WA 98005

Hydro Tech
3929 Aurora Ave N.
Seattle, WA 98015

SEED COMPANIES

Native Seeds/SEARCH
3950 W. Bew York Drive
Tuscon, AZ 85745

Goldsmith Seeds Inc
PO Box 1349
Gilroy, CA 95020

Northrup King
PO Box 1827
Gilroy, CA 95023

Shepherds Garden Seeds
7389 W. Zayante Road
Felton, CA 95018

D. V. Burrell Seed Co.
Box 150
Rocky Ford, CO 81067

Earl May Seed Co
Shenandoah, IA 51603

Blum Seeds
Idaho City Stage
Boise, ID 83707

Natural Food Inst
Box 185 WMB
Dudley, MA 01571

A.H. Hummert Seed Co.
2746 Chouteau Ave.
St. Louis, MO 63103

Sandy Much Herbs
Rt 2 Surrett Cove Road
Leicester, NC 28748

Seedway Inc.
Box 250
Hall, NY 14463

Liberty Seed Co.
PO Box 806
New Philadelphia, OH 44663

Home Orchard Society
PO Box 776
Clackamas, OR 97015

Arco Seed Co.
PO Box 181
El Centro, CA 92244

Heirloom Gardens
Box 138
Guerneville, CA 95446

Petoseed Co.
PO Box 4206
Saticoy, CA 93004

Caprilands Herb Farm
534 Silver St.
Coventry, CT 06238

Nickerson-Zwann
PO Box 19, 2990AA
Baremdrecht, Holland

Henry Field and Co.
407 Sycamore St.
Shenandoah, IA 51602

Burgess Seed Co.
905 Four Seasons Road
Bloomington, IL 61701

Johnny's Selected Seed
Box 299
Albion, ME 04910

Dean Foster Nursery
P.O. Box 548
Hartford, MI 49057

Wyatt-Quarles Seed Co.
Box 739
Garner, NC 27529

Well-Sweep Herb Farm
317 Mt. Bethel Road
Port Murray, NJ 07865

Stokes Seeds
2103 Stokes Bldg.
Buffalo, NY 14240

Wellinger's
2374 W. South Range Rd
North Lima, OH 44452

A.L. Castle Inc.
PO Box 877
Morgan Hill, CA

KUSA Research FD
PO Box 761
Ojai, CA 93023

Royal Sluis Inc.
1293 Harkins Road
Salinas, CA 93901

Chas. C. Hart Seed
PO Box 169
Wethersfield, CT 06109

Sluis & Groot B.V.
PO Box 13   1600 AA
Enkhuisen, Holland

Seed Savers Exchange
203 Rural Avenue
Decorah, IA 52101

R. H. Shumway's
PO Box 777
Rockford, IL 61105

Pinetree Garden Seed
New Gloucester, ME
04260

Orol Ledden and Sons
Center & Atlantic
Sewell, NJ 08080

CORNS
RR 1 Box 32
Tarpon, OK 73950

Reach Seeds
1130 Tetherow Road
Williams, OR 97544

Penn State (Herbs)
906 Wyoming
Forty-Fort PA 18704

Horticultrual Ent.
PO Box 810082
Dallas, TX 75381

Ferry-Morse Seed
PO Box 100
Mnt. View, CA 94042

Le Marche Seeds Intl.
PO Box 566
Dixon, CA 95620

SG Seeds
124 Griffin Street
Salinas, CA 95620

D.A. Posocco
431 W. Main St.
Stafford Sprgs, CT 06076

DeGiorgi Company
Box 413
Council Bluffs, IA 51502

Rogers Brothers Seed
PO Box 80
Idaho Falls, ID 83401

H.G. Hastings
Box 4274
Atlanta, GA 30302

Asgrow Seed Co.
7000 Portage Rd.
Kalamazoo, MI 49001

Leckler's Inc.
13001 Telegraph Road
Lasalle, MI 48415

Thompson & Morgan
Box 1309
Jackson, NJ 08527

Morgan Harris Co.
60 Saginaw Rd
Rochester, NY 14623

DeRuiter Seeds
PO Box 20228
Columbus, OH 43220

Jackson and Perkins
83-A Rose Lane
Medford, OR 97501

SEED COMPANIES, continued

Burpee Seed Co.
300 Park Ave. 9485 B
Warmister, PA 18974

Nichols Garden Nursery
1190 N. Pacific Hwy
Albany, OR 97321

Dixie Plant Farms
PO Box 327
Franklin, VA 23851

Abbott and Cobb
PO Box 307
Feaserville, PA 19047

Gurney Seed Nursery
Yankton, SD57079

Otis Twilley Seed
Box 65
Trevoce, PA 19047

Vermont Bean Seed
Garden Lane
Bomoseen, VT 05732

Geo. W. Park Seed Co.
Box 31, 736 Cokesbury Rd
Greenwood, SC 29647

Wilhite Seed Co.
PO Box 23
Poolville, TX 76076

Northern Nut Growers
4518 Holston Hills Road
Knoxville, TX 37914

Porter and Sons,
Seedsmen
Box 104
Stephenville, TX 76401

Abundant Life Seed Fdn
PO Box 772
Port Townsend, WA 98368

The Cook's Garden
Box 65
Londonderry, VT 05148

Blue Ridge Seed Savers
Box 36
Free Union, VA 22940

Southern Exposure
PO Box 158
North Garden, VA 22959

Le Jardin du Gourmet
West Danville, VT 05873

J. T. Jung Seed Co.
Randolph, WI 53957

HIGH ALTITUDE AND SHORT SEASON NEEDS

High Country Rosarium
1717 Dowing at Park
Denver, CO 80218

Spring River Nursery
Spring River Road
Hartford, MI 49057

Garden City Seeds
PO Box 297
Victor, MT 59875

Good Seed
Box 702
Tonasket, WA 98855

WARM WEATHER SEEDS

Hurov's Tropical Seed
PO Box 1596
Chula Vista, CA 92012

The Banana Tree
715 Northhampton St.
Easton, PA 18042

ORIENTAL MELON AND VEGETABLE SEED

Arco Seed Co.
PO Box 181
El Centro, CA 92244

Petoseed Co.
PO Box 4206
Saticoy, CA 93004

Royal Sluis Inc.
1293 Harkins Road
Salinas, CA 93901

Nickerson-Zwann
PO Box 19   2990 AA
Barendrecht, Holland

Siegers Seed Co
7245 Imlay City Road
Imlay City, MI 48444

Chon and Son
PO Box 251
Malaga, NJ 08328

Penn State Seed
906 Wyoming
Forty-Fort, PA 18074

Park Seed Wholesale
736 Cokesbury Road
Greenwood, SC 29646

SOME CANADIAN SEED COMAPNIES

Alberta Nurseries
BOX 20
Bowden, Alta TOM OKO

Ontario Seed Co, Ltd
Box 144
Waterloo, Ont N2J 3Z9

Vesey's Seeds
York, P.E.I.
COA IPO